Günter

The Dog: A Child's Best Friend

Expert Advice on Mutual Adjustment of Child and Dog

Color photographs:
Christine Steimer

Drawings:
Renate Holzner

Translation from the German:
Elizabeth D. Crawford

BARRON'S

Contents

Double-spread on previous page: *Many children want a dog because they can play with him and tell him everything.*

Growing Up with a Dog 4
Child and Dog: A Great Love 4
Teacher Without Words 6
Fear of Dogs 6
A List of Popular Family Dog Breeds 7
Fear by Example 8
Bad Experiences with Dogs 8
Ways to Overcome the Fear 8
Are There Dangerous Dog Breeds? 8
A Word About "Aggressive" Breeds 9
Why Do Dogs Bite Children? 10
Frequency of Accidents with Dogs 10
Causes of Accidents 11
Analysis of a Specific Example 11
The Reaction of the Dog 12

Learning to Understand Dogs 14
The Dog's Wolf Heritage 14
The Developmental Phases of Puppies 14
The Mentality of the Dog 15
How the Dog "Speaks" 15
The Language of Sound 15
Communicating Through Scent 16
Dominance Ranking 16
Dominance Ranking in the Pack 16
Dominance Ranking in the Family 16
Assertion of Rank 17
HOW-TO: Body Language 18

Advice for Buying 20
Considerations Before Buying 20
The Right Time to Buy 20
The Torture of Choosing 21

A dog fills many roles for a child: playmate, comrade, protector, and comforter.

You Fall in Love with a Mixed Breed 22
If It Should Be a Puppy 22
Deciding on an Older Dog 23
A Dog Has Rights Too 23
The Right Accommodations 23
A Place of Its Own 24
A Healthy Diet 24
Daily Exercise and Play 26
Health Precautions for the Dog 26
What Children Must Respect 27

A Dog in the Family 28
Making the First Contacts 28
The Puppy Arrives 28
The First Days and Nights 28
HOW-TO: Contact with the Dog 30
Don't Rush the Older Dog 32
Getting the Dog Used to a Baby 32
HOW-TO: Playing with the Dog 34
Developing Responsibility in a Child 36
Not Overburdening with Duties 37

Foreword

The Child Refuses to Do His Jobs 37
When the Dog Causes Problems 38
Of Growing Old and Dying 39

Training the Family Dog 40
Obedience Is Important 40
Training Ground Rules 40
HOW-TO: Training 42
Success Achieved in Small Steps 44
Training the Adult Dog 44
Praising and Scolding a Dog
  Correctly 44
Don't Let Bad Behavior Become
  a Habit 45
Dog Schools, Dog Clubs 46

The Child and the Strange Dog 47
Behavior with Strange Dogs 47
The Territorial Behavior of the Dog 47
Barking Dogs Also Bite 47
Contact with Dogs in Their
  Own Territory 48
When Your Child Visits Friends 49
Contact with Dogs on "Neutral
  Ground" 49
HOW-TO: Avoiding Conflicts 50
Playing with Strange Dogs 52
Play Fighting 52
Dogs Tied in Front of Stores 52
Strays 53
When a Dog Becomes Aggressive 54
Careless Dog Owners 54

Small Book of Dog Etiquette 56

Index 60

Useful Addresses and Literature 62

Important Note 63

Dog and child—usually these words signify a great love. The dog is a companion at play, a true friend, and a patient listener to childish dreams and problems. In dealing with the dog, the child develops a sense of responsibility and thus becomes more independent. In view of the positive effects that such a friendship brings with it, you should not set your mind against the innermost desire of the child for a dog in the family. This book will advise you as to when it is the right time to get a dog and how you can structure a harmonious life together for child and dog. Dog expert Gunter Huth thoroughly explains the behavior patterns of dogs and gives advice as to how you and your child or children can avoid conflicts ahead of time. There is a table of "Popular Breeds of Family Dogs" as well as tips on how you can get a dog used to a baby without any problems.

The HOW-TO pages tell how children can make proper contact with the dog at different stages of their life, what games are suitable, and how the family dog should be trained. The "Small Book of Dog Etiquette" lists the important rules for handling a dog.

Brilliant color photographs by Christine Steimer and informative drawings by Renate Hozner show expressly how happy the joint life of a dog and a family can be. The author and the editors of Barron's Educational Series wish you much pleasure with your four-legged friend.

Please read the Important Note on page 63.

Growing Up with a Dog

Were you lucky enough to grow up with a dog? If so, surely you still love to remember those great, honest dog eyes, the soft, cuddly coat, the countless hours of play together, or the happy tricks that you and the dog concocted to play on your parents. But perhaps such experiences were not available to you, although as a child there was nothing your heart desired more than a dog. And perhaps now you would like to make up for your parents' omission and fulfill your children's wish for a dog.

The decision to get a dog: The idea of getting a dog must be considered carefully. Some burning questions may also come up as you proceed to the realization of the idea: What kind of dog would fit into my family? Should I get a dog before a child is planned or is it better to do so after I have children? Could my child perhaps be too young for a dog? Will the dog actually get along well with my child? How can I bring up my child to get along well with either our family pet or a strange dog? Can the dog be dangerous for my child, and how can conflicts be avoided? This book will help you to answer these questions.

A dog in the family: Whatever reasons lead you to resolve to let your child grow up with a dog, it is a good idea and the right decision. Of course you must be fully aware that a dog in the family not only means fun and happiness but also responsibility, duties, work, expense, and perhaps sometimes even trouble.

All of these matters are discussed in this book.

In life with a dog, the good experiences generally outweigh the bad, and the relationship between a child and a dog goes along harmoniously and peacefully. Most certainly your children will also say someday—when they are grown up—"I want my child to grow up with a dog too."

Child and Dog: A Great Love

Is there anything nicer than sharing the joys and sorrows of childhood and youth with a dog? A child and a dog can give much to each other. Not only is the four-legged friend cherished, petted, stroked, cuddled, and loved, but he also becomes a child's confidant; feelings that may be concealed from other children of the same age and parents can be expressed openly to the dog.

The dog as comforter: Joy, excitement, disappointment, grief, and anger, the child can share all with his dog without the animal's talking a lot about it or asking painful questions. The dog is a patient listener. He doesn't interrupt if the childish narration gets too long or confused or if the litany of cares and needs in adolescence is never ending. There is no clever advice about the pangs of first love and the dog doesn't complain when the problems with school grades dominate the discussion. Even the most inane remark is not criticized at all but, at most, honored with a sympathetic whimper.

Somewhat clumsily still, the puppy explores his surroundings. Isn't there anyone to play with?

The girl feels really happy with such a strong protector by her side.

The dog as playmate: Most children want a dog as a faithful, ever-ready companion, who can be involved in role playing, who patiently participates, and who plays, rolls, and tumbles constantly. The family pet wakens the interest of the children to common projects, excites the imagination, and participates in every undertaking without asking any questions about background, meaning, or purpose. The dog always has time and is always interested, and therefore imparts the feeling of trust and loyalty. He gives warmth and closeness, if the child wishes it, and can also offer protection. Most dogs have a natural protective instinct toward children, and the child knows that. This strengthens confidence and independence. Children who grow up with dogs are usually more poised, calmer, and more levelheaded and flexible than others.

This Westie is clearly enjoying having his playmate scratch his stomach.

Teacher Without Words

Dogs teach children important lessons of behavior without words and a pointing finger, and perhaps, therefore, these lessons are imprinted more firmly. To have a dog means to take on responsibility. The dog needs grooming, care, and, in the broadest sense, protection when living in the "pack" with "his" people. A child also understands this very quickly.

Learning responsibility: Children perceive their duties according to how their parents set an example for them and explain the duties to them. In their daily dealing with a pet they learn to understand the animal's requirements, to respect its behavior, and to respond to it appropriately. You can train a child very early to do certain care chores, which vary according to the child's age level (see HOW-TO: Contact with the Dog," pages 30 and 31). The tasks can be expanded with the increasing independence of the child as he grows older. In this way the child learns to take responsibility for a creature that needs protection and to be reliable in undertaking its care.

Developing self-confidence: A child who fulfills the independent tasks in the care of the family dog is strengthened in the feeling of being important and being needed. He is repaid for his efforts with true comradeship—a meaningful success, which strengthens his self-confidence and imprints his character.

Fear of Dogs

The songs of praise are all very well, but what if you are afraid of dogs? Many people avoid getting anywhere near dogs. They cross the street if a dog comes toward them, or when

A List of Popular Family Dog Breeds

Dog Breed	Weight, Size	Character and Requirements
Pomeranian	4–7 lb. (1.8–3 kg) under 10 in. (25 cm)	intelligent, cheerful, devoted; very playful; small but watchful; coat needs daily care
Australian Shepherd	35–70 lb. (25–32 kg) 18–23 in. (53–63 cm)	warm hearted, loving; outstanding "nursemaid," easily trained; breed is one of the shepherd breeds; coat needs regular care
English Springer Spaniel	40–55 lb. (18–25 kg) 19–20 in. (49–51 cm)	easily trained, agreeable; nice with children; cheerful and intelligent; needs lots of exercise; coat needs some care; has hunting drive
Dachshund	11–26 lb. (5–12 kg)	very devoted, especially to children; needs firm training; watchful; coat needs care
French Bulldog	up to 29 lb. (13 kg) about 12 in. (30 cm)	cheerful and pleasant; happy to submit if properly trained; is ready for any fun, watchful but not a barker; coat easy to care for
Golden Retriever	up to 71 lb. (32 kg) 24 in. (62 cm)	friendly, learns easily, good with children, easily trained; not suitable for small apartments; needs activity; has hunting drive; coat needs normal care
Beagle	18–20 lb. (12 kg) 13–15 in. (33–39 cm)	lively, loving, popular family dog; nice with children; watchful but not a barker; strong hunting drive
Maltese	4–7 lb. (1.8–3 kg) up to 10 in. (25 cm)	typical lapdog; devoted to his family; very affectionate and loyal; friendly; coat needs daily care
Pug	up to 18 lb. (8 kg) 12.6 in. (32 cm)	lovable, playful, cheerful, very intelligent; needs much love and returns it; very good with children; needs little exercise; coat easy to care for
Poodle (toy and miniature)	11–14 in. (28–35 cm)	good with children; easily trained, intelligent; nice to keep in an apartment; look for steadiness of character when buying; coat needs care
Sheltie	14–15 in. (35–37 cm)	very intelligent, ready to submit, lovable, gentle; coat needs daily care
Standard Schnauzer	33 lb. (15 kg) 18–20 in. (45–50 cm)	both are cheery, spirited, intelligent; easily trained, very alert; no hunting drive; coat must be trimmed. Standard schnauzers protect their family; the miniature schnauzer is not a lapdog.
Miniature Schnauzer	13–15 lb. (26–27 kg) 12–14 in. (30–35 cm)	

visiting they insist that the family dog be shut up in another room. This fear is based on bad experiences with dogs or is instilled in them by their parents during childhood.

Fear by Example

Children observe carefully what parents and playmates fear. This is how they learn the right way to deal with the things of daily life that actually are dangerous; but at the same time they are also confronted with fears that have no rational basis.

If a mother or father shows a fear of dogs, it won't be long before the child, if only in the drive to imitate, also experiences a revulsion against the animals. In some circumstances he can suffer from it for the rest of his life and pass this fear on to his own children when he is grown up.

▢ My Advice to Parents

Make sure you don't unconsciously and involuntarily instill the fear of dogs in your children through frightened behavior (pulling children away, crossing the street). Become conscious of your own fear response and try to control it. If necessary, let trained experts help you. Never threaten your children with a dog or the "big, bad wolf." Spare them this experience and consciously prepare yourself and your children ahead of time for contact with dogs by taking the advice in this book to heart.

Bad Experiences with Dogs

Anyone who has had a bad experience with a dog is more careful in dealing with these animals in the future. Only in the course of time, if no other negative experiences have occurred, does the aversion for dogs decrease again. However, if the bad experience is connected with a shock (such as a dog attack with biting), an enormous, insurmountable fear is left that can develop into a strong, permanent aversion to dogs.

Ways to Overcome the Fear

Dogs can perceive the fears of humans. This can influence the aggressive behavior of the animal, even if fear alone isn't enough to make a friendly dog aggressive. However, dogs clearly seem to know when people are afraid of them.

Overcoming the fear: If you suffer from a great fear of dogs, you should not simply accept this as fate. Work to free yourself of the anxiety either with professional help or with self-therapy by following my advice below. It will then be easier for you not to show fear of dogs in front of your children. Avoid bringing up your children with the idea that all dogs are vicious and dangerous.

▢ My Advice to Parents

Do not suppress your fear. Purposely seek contact with well-mannered dogs that you are acquainted with—for instance, in the neighborhood, with friends, or with relatives. Feel your way, but be firm with yourself. Endure the presence of the dog and also practice touching it. You will soon see how nice it is to pet a dog. Accompany the dog owner on a walk and provide yourself with as many positive experiences as possible. The result could be that you yourself will buy a dog who will quickly remove the last shred of your doubts through his trust and affection.

Are There Dangerous Dog Breeds?

Parents who have not yet had any experience with dogs will ask anxiously whether there are dangerous breeds.

A walk with "his" human pack gives the dog the most pleasure.

Certainly the threshhold of irritability is lower in some breeds than in others, but no breed can be graded ahead of time as either dangerous or as completely harmless. The decisive factor is always the genes of the parent animals. If both parents of a puppy are aggressive, the puppy probably also has the genetic inheritance to be aggressive. The breeder can promote this tendency or suppress it through the choice of the parents. Therefore, you should only buy a dog from a responsible breeder and should observe the parent animals carefully (see "If It Should Be a Puppy," page 22).

A Word About "Aggressive" Breeds

In the media the dogs belonging to the "aggressive" breeds (like Bull Terriers, Pit Bulls, Rottweilers, Bull Mastiffs, and others) are always characterized as "bloodthirsty beasts" and as a danger to life and limb whenever they turn up. In all fairness, some things need to be clarified.

Their original role: Certain dog breeds were originally bred especially for ferocity and were used for guarding/fighting against other dogs and wild animals like bears, wolves, and mountain lions. The demand made of such a dog was that it absolutely possess the desire to fight and protect, even if it meant fighting to its own death. Because such acute aggressiveness does not exist in ordinary dogs, dog breeders chose to breed out any hindering characteristics, such as a lack of aggressiveness toward other animals, intolerance of pain, and so forth.

"Aggressive" breeds as family pets: For many decades most so-called "aggressive" dog breeds have been bred responsibly, and the undue aggressive behavior that was originally present was, in most cases, again returned to normal levels. If they come from a good breeder, such dogs can usually be quite peaceful and good with children. With correct handling, good training, and common sense they can be good family pets with no need for undue concern.

The use, abuse, and misuse of aggressive breed dogs: Regrettably, in recent times the misuse of the "aggressive breeds" has clearly been increasing. Deliberately, some unwise people are striving to breed dangerous dogs out of otherwise usually peaceable breeds. Sadly, these people are finding a growing market. Dogs bred specifically for aggressiveness always present a danger. They are very hard to control, extremely aggressive toward other dogs, and a menace to the community. Such dogs are unpredictable, not unlike canine time bombs. Neither bodily pain nor wounds keep them from pursuing the attack. They have been created for fighting to the death.

Deliberately producing an unsafe dog is a blight on all other dogs and all responsible dog owners. The breeding of dogs with good temperaments, in ALL breeds, must always remain the primary dog breeding principle.

Why Do Dogs Bite Children?

Dog attacks on people are often exaggerated in the media. The impression is made that dog attacks happen often and are almost always connected with considerable injury. Fortunately this isn't so.

Frequency of Accidents with Dogs

While any dog bite to a child, or an adult, is one too many, it is not true that most such bites result in terrible phsyical and mental traumas. If one grows up around dogs, lives around dogs, and enjoys the company of dogs, there are going to be some nips and bites along the way. The overwhelming majority of these are accidental, done by a startled, frightened, or injured pet. Most such bites don't break the skin and few require medical treatment. Most such instances are not reported and sometimes not even remembered. More serious bites usually occur when a child or adult is somewhere they shouldn't be or doing something they shouldn't be doing. Under adult supervision, away from territory or objects that a dog considers its own (like its food bowl), most dogs are not candidates to bite anyone.

Leash laws and some training for adults and children will prevent most confrontations that could result in a dog attack. Correct human behavior arround dogs will eliminate most incidental bites. Good dog training and control will stop most other attacks. Common sense when strange or stray dogs are encountered will keep such accidents from happening.

Causes of Accidents

Usually the background details remain unclear in press reports describing the attacks of dogs on children. When the incidents are examined more closely by experts, it very often becomes evident that human misbehavior in some form was the cause of the animal's overreaction. In fact, more often than you think, adults and children overstep the dog's limits of tolerance. The animals are teased, kicked, annoyed, and beaten; territorial requirements are simply ignored. Even if the actions are done unintentionally or happen out of thoughtlessness and ignorance of correct human behavior, it is still astonishing how patiently most dogs put up with these "impertinances" without responding aggressively.

Analysis of a Specific Example

Let me illustrate with an example of a thoroughly ordinary situation of children's misbehavior in dealing with dogs.

The case: An eight-year-old girl, by herself, is walking a mixed-breed dog the size of a Boxer on a leash. Suddenly, the child, for no apparent reason, begins to scold the dog, who has been walking along well-behaved at her heel. When the animal doesn't react and continues to trot along faithfully beside her, the girl hits the dog on the head with her hand. The blows are not especially hard, but it is clear that the child isn't caressing the dog and wants to reprimand it. The dog tolerates the blows without a sign of aggression.

The analysis: You don't need to know dogs especially well to be able to imagine that this situation could also have turned out very differently. The analysis produces the following criticisms:

• It is irresponsible of the parents to send a small child with a dog of this size out on the street alone.

• If the dog were to pull on the leash with all his weight, the child would not be capable of holding the animal. The child could fall, be injured, or even be dragged into the path of traffic. A reason for such dog behavior could be the sighting of another dog passing along the sidewalk on the other side of the street or a cat running away.

• What would happen if the child were spoken to by a stranger and the dog thought he had to protect her? The girl would never be able to control the dog's natural reaction with her own strength.

• Another criticism is the way the child handles the dog. Dogs are social beings who are born into a society and are furnished for community life

A Bull Terrier from a good breeding line is nice with children and very playful.

11

Fun is apparently all these three have in mind.

with certain behavior patterns. From the point of view of the dog, he occupies an established position within the family, as do "his" people (see "Dominance Ranking in the Family," page 16).

The Reaction of the Dog

If the rules of ranking had been overstepped in the case presented above, the outcome may have been different in any one of the following ways.

• The dog treated the child as an adult dog would have treated a puppy: he patiently permitted the behavior in the above example because he classified the blows as immature puppy behavior. However, the dog's attitude can change from one day to the next, as soon as he gets the impression that the child has outgrown "puppy age" and from now on has to be taken seriously. But how shall it make this "change of mind" visible so that it can be unmistakeably recognized by all members of the family?

• The dog regards the child as of equal rank; he ignores the blows, is very tolerant and of steady character, and does not the regard the blows as an attack on his position. If he should consider his place in the order of dominance threatened, he may react with growls. If the blows are not stopped, a nip can be the result. This is painful, to be sure, but not a bite in any real sense.

• The dog regards the child as being of lower rank. If she doesn't understand his warning growl, the dog can now nip somewhat harder or even bite in order to make his position clear in the order of dominance.

12

Will this mousehole ever make good on its promise and yield the desired "contents"?

My Advice to Parents

Even if it is understandable why the dog reacts in a certain way in certain situations, the fact still remains that even nips can be painful and can often leave bruises or bite marks. Much worse yet are the psychological consequences of the shock at the beloved dog's suddenly snapping. Some children never get over such a shocking experience. Therefore, show your little children early and consistently how to treat an animal so that conflicts are avoided. Teach your children to love animals and to have the necessary respect for every living creature with patience, understanding, and capacity for empathy.

Learning to Understand Dogs

The genes of her wild ancestor, the wolf, still slumber in the dog. When you know the typical behavior patterns of your dog, you will understand her better.

In order to live with a dog in harmony and without any problems it is important to become familiar with the animal's nature. In the first place, situations that are dangerous for children occur when parents do not understand how to prepare their children to deal properly with dogs. If you want to understand dogs, you must know where their roots are, how their sphere of emotional perceptions is structured, and how—and above all, why—they react to some particular impressions one way and not another.

The Dog's Wolf Heritage

All dog breeds—from the smallest Chihuahua to the biggest Mastiff—are descended from the wolf. About fifteen thousand years ago humans began to domesticate the wolf, and over the course of thousands of years a great variety of dog breeds arose through strict breeding selection from a single ancient form . Since then a close relationship has developed between people and dogs. Nevertheless, in her very innermost reaches, the dog has remained a predator, and this wolf inheritance is clearly expressed in many behavior patterns.

My Advice to Parents

If you already have a dog or want to get one, you should thoroughly come to terms with your animal's development, behavior, and forms of expression. This way you are best able to explain to your children how to handle the dog successfully.

The Developmental Phases of Puppies

In the first three months after birth, every dog goes through distinct developmental phases, which determine her behavior in later life. This so-called imprinting takes place in several time-limited and irretrievable phases. Experiences that are missing or are negative during this time are very difficult or often impossible to make up for later.

Newborn phase (first to second week): The puppy comes into the world blind and deaf. On her own she finds her mother's nipple, on which she is completely dependent during this period.

Transitional phase (second to third week): The eyes and ears are open now and the puppy makes her first attempts at walking. After the third week the teeth come through.

Imprinting phase (fourth to seventh week): The senses of sound and smell are imprinted, and the eyes begin to follow movement. The puppy becomes more active and begins to make short excursions into her surroundings. At about seven weeks the puppy is weaned by the mother. In play with her mother and littermates she learns social behavior patterns. It is important that the puppy have enough contact with other dogs and humans during this phase so that she will later get along well with others of her species and develop a trusting relationship with people.

Socialization phase (eighth to twelfth week): The close contact with littermates becomes looser, and the puppy becomes more and more independent. This is the ideal time for the young dog to join her future family.

Ranking phase (from the twelfth week): The young dog endeavors to fit into a certain rank in the "human pack" (see "Dominance Ranking in the Family," page 16). All the experiences gained during this learning phase determine the puppy's later behavior in the family. Therefore, the training of the dog should also begin now (see "HOW-TO: Training," pages 42 and 43).

The Mentality of the Dog

To properly evaluate the behavior of your four-legged friend, you should know how the dog sensorily perceives humans and her environment.

Nose: The dog's scenting capability is vastly superior to that of humans. Therefore, the dog is often termed a "sniffing animal." Your pet's nose is her best-developed sensory organ and, at the same time also the most important. So, first of all, the dog gets a "picture" of her environment through her nose. Every dog owner has observed the great interest with which his four-legged companion sniffs new objects, strange dogs, and unknown people.

Ears: A dog hears markedly better than a human. Therefore, the dog can also hear softly spoken commands well. On the other hand, your pet is also sensitive to shrill noises like children screaming, loud radio music, and the like.

Eyes: The color perception of the dog is somewhat limited, to be sure, but she sees better than humans in poor light conditions. Aside from this, the dog can only perceive objects well when they move or if she herself moves. Therefore, she can react extraordinarily fast to things that move suddenly or in an unfamiliar way.

How the Dog "Speaks"

Every dog masters the "international language" of her fellow dogs, which consists of olfactory, visual, and acoustic information. She uses the same signals in dealing with humans. Therefore, you should understand your four-legged friend's means of expression and be able to interpret them correctly. You also need to explain to your children how the dog "speaks." Thus, wrong reactions to a dog can be avoided.

The Language of Sound

Dogs express their frame of mind and their wishes with a variety of sound utterances.

Barking can mean a declaration of joy or an invitation to play. But barking also occurs as a warning or as a sign of fear and uneasiness.

Growling is a serious threat, which is used in signalling possible attack or defense.

Whimpering expresses submission or pain. It also is used in begging for food or as a demand for play.

Puppies practice typical behavior patterns in their play.

15

Howling signals loneliness and goes back to the wolf heritage, because a member separated from the pack makes himself known that way.

Crying and squealing are signs of anxiety or pain. Puppies, especially, use these sounds to attract attention.

Communicating through Scent

Sniffing: Dogs take in all the important information about their environment through their nose. They eagerly sniff everything. They especially find interesting the feces and scent markings of their fellow dogs, which they "read" like a newspaper. A dog also knows how to interpret the scents of the human: she smells whether someone is friendly, anxious, or angry.

Marking: Male dogs stake out their territory by urinating on marking spots like trees or house corners. Passing males sniff these "visiting cards" and cover the scent of the previous one with their own scent. Female dogs only mark their territory with urine when they are in heat in order to attract males.

Dominance Ranking

Every dog has the desire to insert herself into a dominance order, whether she finds herself in a pack of other dogs or in a family of people. This desire is innate and is inherited from the dog's wild ancestors, the wolves.

Dominance Ranking in the Pack

Among wolves there is a strict hierarchy, which must be observed by all members of the pack. At the top is the lead wolf, who largely determines the hunting and resting periods and leads the pack. Then the other members of the pack are arranged under the lead wolf in descending ranks. Puppies are only under the protection of their mother until the age of about four months; then they must find their own place in the society. The young wolves secure their rank by mock fights with their littermates and the other lower-ranking members of the pack. However, these ranks do not hold for all their lives. Any wolf can rise or fall in rank during the course of its life.

Dominance Ranking in the Family

In accordance with this wild heritage, the family dog also has the need to insert herself into the dominance order. She is thus automatically transferring her behavior patterns to the family. The family pet clearly feels the leadership position of the parents, which is established by their role as providers of life-essential care. In the same way, the dog recognizes the dependence and the helplessness of the children. From her point of view, she thus classifies one of the parents—usually the one who takes primary responsibility for her training—as the "lead dog." All other "members of the pack" are subordinate to this "lead dog." Now the dog must still establish her own position, which usually develops as follows:

• The dog subordinates herself completely to the "lead dog" (whether master or mistress), likewise to the next-ranking (adult) in the family.

• Older children from the age of about twelve are regarded by the dog as equal in rank. She treats them friendly as a rule and accords them the same rights, as long as she doesn't feel that they are competing with her for her rank.

• Younger children, under 12, are regarded by the dog as subordinates,

ranking below him. How much liberty they may take with him depends on his tolerance, and it varies from dog to dog. If the lower-ranking child oversteps the limits of the dog's tolerance, it can happen that the dog will put him in his place (see below).
• Small children up to the age of five have special rights, because they are ranked by the dog as puppies. They are, of course, subordinate to her, but they enjoy a certain "fool's safety" and may overstep the bounds somwhat with the (higher-ranking) dog before she employs "training measures." The measure of this freedom likewise depends on the dog's personality.

Assertion of Rank

If the dog feels that her position is challenged by another of lower rank, she will defend her position, even within the "family pack."

What parents should watch out for: Sometimes, sheerly in high spirits, children lose the feeling for when they are going too far. Therefore, keep an eye on your child when he plays or romps with the dog. Things like pulling the dog by the coat or the ears or the tail should of course be taboo, because they hurt the dog. Also, the child shouldn't give any commands to the dog, because these demand strict submission to someone not entitled to it because of his rank. As a rule, the dog clearly shows when her limit of tolerance has been reached. No matter whether the dog growls or whines, lays her ears back and tucks in her tail, or even growls and shows her teeth, the treatment that has ignited this reaction must be ended immediately. The dog should never be so provoked that she feels it necessary to nip.

The strange dog is sniffed from all sides.

The overbite on the muzzle controls the puppy.

Puppies learn for life by tussling and playing.

HOW-TO: Body Language

The dog expresses her moods with the help of body language much more often than through sound. In body language, the way she holds her body, ears, and tail are important, as well as her gestures. Help your children learn "dog language," and explain to them the different ways dogs behave and express themselves.

Friendly Mood
Friendliness is expressed with the body held low, pronounced tail wagging, ears laid back, and whining or whimpering.

Implication for the family: If the dog exhibits this behavior, she wants to cuddle and be petted. In this agreeable mood she can be introduced to small children, and they can be led by the hand to learn how to pet the dog.

Invitation to Play
Drawing 1
The dog invites play by laying her front paws flat on the floor and raising her rear end. At the same time she shows her "play face," with the jaws slightly opened, the upper lip pulled back, and the ears laid back. Often she will also bark joyfully.

Implication for the family: In this playful mood, depending on the dog's temperament, she will tend toward exuberance and vigorous motion. The strength of the dog will become an issue. You should stay with children up to six years old while they play with the dog so they don't get knocked down.

Anxious Mood
Drawing 2
If the dog is afraid, she will hold her body down and lay her ears back. Her head will be sunk and the tail will be tucked between her hind legs.

Implication for the family: Within the "family pack," abject fear should usually be unknown to the dog. If you ever scold your dog, she will most likely press herself to the floor in front of you. The dog isn't showing you fear so much as humbleness and complete submission. Don't scold her anymore at this point. A dog pushed into real fear may bite because she doesn't know any other way out of the situation.

"Anxiety biters": If dogs have had little contact with humans during the imprinting phase (see "Developmental Phases of Puppies," page 14), they remain shy and usually run around with their tails tucked in. Since they are constantly under stress, they snap easily because of fear. Such dogs don't belong in a family with children! If your dog shows such behavior after you have bought it, you should

2 Clear signs of fear: lowered body, ears laid back, tucked-in tail.

place it in an adult-only home—even if it is a very difficult decision for you.

Display Behavior
A displaying dog stands with legs stiff, tail held high, and back hairs ruffed up so as to appear as large as possible. The ears are upright and pointed forward and the gaze is rigid. Male dogs display to each other in order to establish who is the superior. If both feel equally strong, the display can

1 This posture invites the mistress or master to play with the dog.

turn into threatening movements and even a fight.

Implication for the family: The dog doesn't show this behavior in the family, as a rule. If the dog should display to another dog while being walked, it can lead to a fight. Keep children far away from the dog in such situations (see "Play Fighting," page 52).

Submission
Drawing 3

In active submission, also called "social greeting," the lower-ranking animal demonstrates friendliness to the higher-ranking one. The body posture is somewhat relaxed and a lowered tail is wagging quickly. The corners of the mouth are pulled back and the ears are laid back.

Implication for the family: When the dog shows these signals, she wants to lick the hands and faces of "her" people. This behavior derives from puppyhood, when the puppy, by licking the fangs of the mother dog, animates her to regurgitate food for her.

4 This posture advises caution: With tail stiffly erect, neck fur on end, and teeth bared, the dog threatens his opponent.

In passive submission, the dogs lies on her back and presents her neck and belly (see drawing 3). With ears laid back and tail tucked under, eye contact with the opponent is avoided. This behavior as a rule induces an inhibition against biting in the stronger dog and the fight is ended or avoided without injury.

Implication for the family: When the dog rolls on her back in front of people and tucks her tail under, it means deep trust and security. You or your children should stroke the dog and speak kindly to her when she displays this behavior.

3 The weaker one signals submission. The stronger one breaks off his attack.

Signals before Attack
Drawing 4

Before a dog attacks, she threatens her opponent, whether it be another dog or a human.

Warning ritual: The dog will make of herself appear larger to impress her target. Her tail is kept stiffly upright, without wagging. Her neck hair will be fluffed, teeth will be bared, and she will growl (see drawing 4).

Implication for the family: The dog is irritated and shows that she has reached the limit of her tolerance. Whatever behavior has produced this reaction should be discontinued immediately.

Attack: If a threatening dog is irritated further, she may proceed to attack.

Implication for the family: The dog will only attack a member of the "family pack" if she is severely irritated or if she places herself at the top in the order of dominance. In any case, this behavior requires action by the family (see "When the Dog Causes Problems," page 38).

Advice on Buying

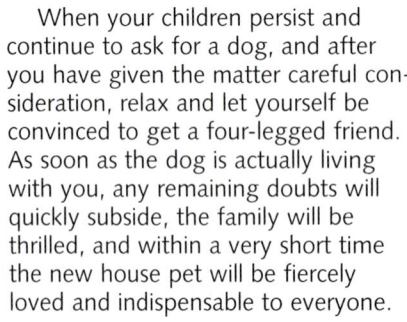

When your children persist and continue to ask for a dog, and after you have given the matter careful consideration, relax and let yourself be convinced to get a four-legged friend. As soon as the dog is actually living with you, any remaining doubts will quickly subside, the family will be thrilled, and within a very short time the new house pet will be fiercely loved and indispensable to everyone.

Considerations Before Buying
When parents and children decide to take on the responsibility of a dog, they must also be able to commit to it for the long term. The normal life expectancy of a dog is somewhere between ten and fifteen years. You should never buy a dog on the spur of the moment just because you are in the mood!

The following list of questions should help you make the decision as to whether a dog is the right pet for your family.
• Do you know the requirements of your future pet? Every type of dog has special needs that you must fulfill. To avoid any surprises, you should definitely find out ahead of time about the characteristics and special qualities of the breed you want.
• Can you guarantee daily optimal care of the dog? Do you have enough time to take him for walks, to care for his coat, and for daily activities with him? A dog should not be left alone for anymore than is absolutely necessary each day.

• Are you ready to be responsible for the care of the dog all by yourself someday? Even if your children swear eagerly to be responsible for the dog's care, the moment can come when all or a large part of the care falls to the parents.
• Do you have enough time in the first few months to train the dog? This is exclusively the task of the parents, not the children.
• Does your landlord allow dogs? Read your lease to find out. Also inform your neighbors ahead of time about the planned "increase in family."
• Can you guarantee that your dog will be well cared for if you ever go on vacation without him? Ask relatives or friends if they would be willing to let you leave him in their care during that time.
• Is anyone in your family allergic to animal hair? Clear this with your doctor before the animal comes into the house.
• Are you ready to undertake the expense of dog licensing, food, care equipment, and visits to the veterinarian? Certain kinds of dogs may affect the kind of insurance you should carry.
• Is the dog still going to be well cared for in ten or fifteen years? Your job situation may change enough to make it difficult for you to care for the dog. In addition, your children will be older and more responsible, but they may be busy with school or their jobs, too. Who will take care of the dog?

The Right Time to Buy
Normally it isn't a problem to integrate a dog into a family structure that

He not only looks perky, he is! Now the only thing missing is the right playmate to romp with and chase.

Dogs are social creatures. They want to be part of things at all times in all places.

is already established. But wait until your youngest child is well able to understand simple behavioral rules about handling the dog. This should be the case at around three years old. With a younger child there is always a danger that the two curious creatures will clash with one another, which can do mutual harm to their need to explore.

Example: The dog can be frightened by a loud noise from the child and nip the child. This bad experience with the dog (see page 8) embeds itself in the child's mind and can produce a fear of dogs. On the other hand, the child can repeatedly grab for the eyes of the dog or roughly pull on his coat or ears. The dog may possibly develop a lasting aversion to children.

The Torture of Choosing

Perhaps you are already thinking of a particular breed whose looks please you or that is associated with happy childhood memories. Keep in mind that your future pet should fit into your family. Therefore, it is recommended that ahead of time you read thoroughly any pertinent literature about the nature, special character, and requirements of the desired breed. The dog's requirements should also be fulfilled, however. So it doesn't make sense to get a hunting or guard dog if he can't keep as busy as he needs to. If you haven't settled on a particular breed, you are faced with the hard task of choosing the right dog out of the multitude of dog breeds. In that case, also consider your children's "favorites," and let them have a part in the decision.

My Advice to Parents

Choose a breed whose nature and temperament fit well into your family and living conditions.

- A large, bouncing dog (for instance, a retriever) should not be penned up in a city apartment and, a short-legged dog with a long back (for instance, a dachshund) should not be kept in a fourth-floor walk-up. Best suited for small city apartments are small to medium-sized dogs, while larger dogs seem to do best in a house with a yard.
- Also factor in your own requirements when making the choice of a dog breed. People who aren't keen on spending a lot of extra time outdoors are better off with a dog that is somewhat more easygoing. On the other hand, for a sports-oriented family that goes in for a lot of outdoor activities, a rugged dog who joyfully participates in all undertakings is outstanding.
- Above all, choose a family dog that likes children, that is good-natured, playful, and robust (see "Popular Family Dog Breeds," page 7). Oversensitive, nervous dogs that are disturbed

This is the right way to carry a puppy: One hand supports the rear end while the other supports the back.

by noise are in the wrong place when they are in a family with children.

You Fall in Love with a Mixed Breed

There is nothing wrong with mixed breeds. Usually they are faithful, clever, adaptable, and robust animals, who fit very well into a family. But since the different breed characteristics in any mixed-breed animal are only partially expressed, particular qualities of character cannot be determined with certainty. Once in a while "several souls struggle in one breast," which could result in a somewhat unpredictable pet.

If It Should Be a Puppy

If you decide on a puppy, the whole family can have a part in all the developmental and life stages of the dog. In this way one learns the characteristic features, ways of expression, and requirements of the animal very precisely. However, you will need much time, patience, and understanding until the little animal is housebroken and properly trained.

You should never buy a puppy in a hurry! Get information about serious breeders of the desired breed from the American Kennel Club (see "Organizations," page 62). A good breeder lets his dogs grow up living in direct daily contact with the family and not in a kennel away from the house. He will gladly show you the puppies and the mother dog. All the dogs should be clean and well cared for and their behavior toward the breeder should be relaxed and free of fear. A serious breeder will find the best possible homes for his puppies. Therefore, accept his questions about how the puppy will live with you.

Note: Place special importance on only buying a dog from a breeder who regularly brings his puppies into contact with children. Only when the dog has had good experiences with children in earliest puppyhood is he best suited for life as a family pet.

Choosing your puppy: Rely on the advice of the breeder. He knows the puppies and can, even now, predict the qualities of their future character in outline. He will certainly recommend the puppy most suitable for you. The puppy should then come home to live with you at the age of eight to ten weeks.

My Advice to Parents

If you choose to buy a puppy from a pet store, be sure that the store is clean and that the animals are healthy. In addition, the pet store owner or manager should be knowledgeable about the pets that he sells and should be able to provide you with the same information that a breeder would supply to you.

Deciding on an Older Dog

Getting an adult dog may not be advisable if your children are under ten years old. The adaptability and learning ability of a dog lessens with increasing age. Above all, if the animal has not been used to the company of children, it will have difficulty getting used to the new situation. This is mainly because older dogs already have behind them experiences and adventures by which they were imprinted, not only as puppies but also in their entire earlier lives (see "Developmental Phases of Puppies," page 14).

Dogs from the animal shelter are often the victims of a sad past, which sometimes expresses itself in their behavior. Thus, if you want an animal from a shelter, you should only choose an animal if you are certain that it has a good-humored, gentle nature and likes children. Such a dog will, generally, also reward "his" family with a high degree of affection and loyalty.

A Dog Has Rights Too

A dog has come to live with you. Now begins a wonderful period, rich in excitement and and new experiences, that will enliven the whole family. Love and understanding alone, however, are not enough to provide the dog with a happy life. Every dog has rights, too, which express themselves in his needs and requirements. And it is imperative—for the parents, as well as for the children—to recognize, fulfill, and respect them.

The Right Accommodations

Even before they get the dog, the family must be clear about how and where the new pet is going to live.

House or apartment: The greatest enrichment for the entire family and the animal is if the dog is allowed to live in the middle of his "human pack" in the apartment or house. Many daily experiences thus demand his attention and require a corresponding reaction to it. On the other hand, the constant shared life with an animal is also a great gain for the family. Children then have the best opportunity to observe their pet, interpret his moods and learn to understand them, and develop a deep bond with him.

Keeping the dog in a doghouse: Only if the dog spends most of his time in the house with the family does it not harm him to stay in the doghouse at night. As a rule, even in the family pack not much happens at night. Living only in a doghouse, however, is not appropriate, because the dog misses the close contact with "his" people. Puppies and young dogs should always have family contact, because they need close contact with "their" humans for their development.

Keeping the dog on a chain is, in reality, torture for the animal and should be strictly avoided for this reason Dogs mistreated this way often become behaviorally disturbed and a danger to human society.

A Place of Its Own

The dog needs his own place, possibly a crate or carrier, in the house or apartment. It is here that he passes the night, rests during the day, and can also gnaw undisturbed on a dog biscuit or a rawhide knot once in a while. The dog's crate is his bed, his "personal territory," and his kingdom. When he withdraws there, he shows that he wants to rest and be left alone. Children and adults must understand this and respect it. They shouldn't disturb him anymore, urge him to play, or try to pull him out of his own special place.

Location: Arrange the crate for your dog in a quiet, draft-free corner of the room, from which the animal can observe the entire room. Dogs are distinctly curious and want to see what's going on around them. The crate should not be too close to the heating apparatus in the home because it can easily become too warm for the dog.

Equipment: Whether you buy a crate or airline-type carrier from the pet store it should be big enough for the dog to stretch out comfortably in it. Buy it with the adult dog in mind. Partitions can keep the size appropriate for a puppy and then be removed as the animal grows.

Carpet remnants cut to fit or washable cushions make suitable linings for the bed. There are also special liners, which are sold in pet stores.

A Healthy Diet

For the dog, eating is an important part of life. Even as a puppy he learns to push through his littermates and defend his food. He will also do this in his family pack. Therefore, explain to your children that they absolutely must leave the dog alone when he is eating and under no circumstances attempt to take his dish away from him. He should not get the feeling that he has to defend his food against the children.

An established feeding place is important. Thus, the dog knows that here he will be fed—always at the same time—and there will always be a dish of fresh water there for him.

Puppies need a special puppy diet (from the pet store), which is divided into several small portions per day. When you get your little dog, the breeder will give you the first instructions for feeding. Doubtless he will also give you a small supply of the food that the puppy is used to. This way you avoid too abrupt a change of diet, which in some dogs leads to digestive problems.

"Dangling is fun. If you fall, you can grab me."

Adult dogs are often fed once a day. The dog should rest after eating and not rush about. Therefore, it's a sound idea to feed the dog in the evening when the body has the whole night to digest the food. You can also divide the food into two portions during the day, for instance a smaller portion in the morning and main part of it in the evening.

My tip: The simplest thing is to feed with ready-made dog food, since it is extraordinarily difficult to prepare a healthy, well-balanced food mixture with all the nutrients, vitamins, and minerals necessary for the dog yourself.

Daily Exercise and Play

Exercise is one of the dog's most elementary requirements. This is easy to understand, because the ancestors of the house dog, the wolves, are coursing animals that hunt in packs. In general, not only are there avid runners among the multitude of the different dog breeds, but playful species are also represented, all the way up to the comfortably lazy ones. Thus, today any dog owner can find the animal that fits his own requirements.

Worn out from many games with "his" children, the dachshund is entitled to a short rest in his basket.

Sufficient daily exercise is needed by every dog for the dog to remain fit and healthy. Therefore, there should be enough time scheduled every day for walks and play. During this time, your children can also be very active, because their needs for exercise aren't much less than those of the dog (see "HOW-TO: Playing with the Dog," pages 34 and 35). At least once a day a longer walk (about an hour) in which the animal has enough opportunity to sniff and romp should be undertaken.

How much exercise the dog needs depends on the breed and the training condition. A longhaired, heavy dog like, perhaps, the Bernese mountain dog is not suited for high-performance sport, rather, he prefers leisurely hiking. Also, very small, short-legged breeds do better on a walk than on a speedy bicycle expedition. Carefully observe your dog and you will soon find out how much exercise he needs.

Health Precautions for the Dog

A dog from good stock is usually robust and not susceptible to illness. As a prerequisite for his healthy maintenance he needs the right food, enough exercise, good care, and a great deal of affection. Also extremely important are regular preventive measures, such as worming and immunizations. At regular intervals your veterinarian will vaccinate against rabies, distemper, hepatitis, leptospirosis, parvovirus, and other ailments that can be fatal to a dog. In much of the United States, dog owners are also encouraged to give regular doses of heartworm preventives. The veterinarian can also use this opportunity to examine the dog and assess its general health.

Recognizing signs of illness: Naturally the dog can become ill once in a while in spite of the best care. If he suddenly exhibits a change of behavior or has no desire to eat, it could be the first signs of illness. Here children are often the best observers, because they are occupied with the dog a great deal on a daily basis. Teach your children to report any changes in the dog's behavior to you immediately. Then observe your dog carefully and, if necessary, consult a veterinarian.

What Children Must Respect

- The child must learn that the dog has needs and requirements as an independent creature that it is essential to respect. A dog is not an inanimate toy that always functions when the child wants him to but a playmate with certain rights. If the dog indicates that he has had enough of playing and romping together, the child must accept it.
- When the dog retires to his crate, he wants to be left alone. It's all the same whether he is asleep, dozing, or gnawing on his bone; the child should leave him in peace and not try to get him to play anymore.
- As long as the dog is eating or drinking, the child may not disturb him. He should never take away a filled food dish or a bone, since the dog might decide to defend his property.
- When the dog withdraws with his favorite toy, the child should not take it away from him.
- If the dog ever shows himself not to be in top form, if he is sick, injured, or in pain, the child must respect his increased need for rest. Reassuring, parentally supervised, petting is all right, of course.

A Dog in the Family

Making the First Contacts

The first encounter of child and dog should take place in accordance with the developmental age of the child. Even before the future household pet arrives in the family, a "sniffing visit" can help to establish the first contact between child and dog and produce empathy.

Child and puppy: If your child is three years old, you should take her to the breeder or the animal shelter when you choose the puppy. The child will love to see the group of little dogs and the visit will definitely be an opening for an explanation about the needs of the animals. It doesn't hurt if your child strokes the puppies or carries them in her arms. An older child, from about six years old, can already help to pick out the future family dog.

Child and older dog: An adult dog from the animal shelter should only come into the family if your child is at least ten years old. Also, your child absolutely should be there to choose the dog. So even at the first visit to the animal shelter you can see whether child and dog "smell good" to each other. This is especially important with an older dog, because he will need a somewhat longer acclimation time in the new family (see "Deciding on an Older Dog," page 23).

The first meeting with the dog: Explain to your child that she should approach the dog quietly and slowly at the first meeting and should then hold out the back of her hand so that the dog can sniff it. Impress on your child that she must not scream loudly or "squeal with excitement." Otherwise the dog could snap in shock or fear. Of course the animal must also not be pulled by the ears, tail, or coat or irritated in any other way.

The Puppy Arrives

Finally the day comes when the puppy is brought home. The homecoming day is a drastic experience for the puppy, because she is separated from her mother and littermates for the first time. You can make getting acclimated easier for the puppy if you give the breeder one of your old pieces of clothing a few weeks before you pick up the little one. The breeder gives this to the puppy in the nesting box so that it takes on the familiar smell of the pack.

Transport home: If your child is five years old or older, you should take her with you to get the puppy. But explain ahead of time that she has to keep very quiet in order not to upset the little animal even more. Take another adult along with you. Then one adult can drive while the other holds the little dog on his lap. The dog can lie on the piece of clothing that she already knows. Wrapped in the familiar scent of her old pack, she will get through the journey very well. For a long trip, plan stops about every hour.

The First Days and Nights

Cautious acclimation: At the beginning, the puppy needs time and rest to get used to her new home. You should

Sitting together in the doghouse is a wonderful way to concoct the next caper.

The dog as a "baby-sitter." He carefully watches over the newest addition to the family.

guarantee her both. Put the familiar piece of clothing in her crate or carrier right after she arrives, then put the puppy in the crate, and leave her alone. Explain to your children that they should only observe the newcomer quietly and shouldn't rush right up to her.

It won't be long before the puppy has processed her first impressions and gotten curious enough to explore her new home and pack. Even if it is certainly very hard on your children not to be able to play with her now that the long-desired puppy is finally here, the basic rule is that the initiative for common play and action should belong to the dog in the first weeks. Then later it happens all by itself.

HOW-TO: Contact with the Dog

The Dog Is Not a Plaything

This statement is the most fundamental principle in the relationship between a child and dog. Playthings are inanimate objects without feelings or will of their own with which children can do what they want. A dog, or any other animal, is exactly the opposite. Anyone who completely turns a puppy over to a child is acting irresponsible to the utmost degree and may be sowing the seeds of later misfortune. The blame for future problems is not the child's, not at all the dog's, but the parents' alone!

With proper treatment the dog can become something that is much nicer and more valuable than a toy: a true, loyal friend, a creature that one—of course always respecting the dog's rights as an animal—can involve wonderfully in games. This relationship rewards both the child and the dog.

Dog and Child at Different Age Levels

Contact with the dog turns out differently depending on the age and maturity of the child. The early watchfulness of the parents, which is utterly essential when a small child encounters the dog, softens over the course of years to the confidence and the knowledge that the child is under good

1 Small children should be introduced to the dog cautiously.

care in the company of the dog, that in her he has a terrific playmate, a watchful protector, and a true friend who is enthusiastic for every game and is always there when she is needed.

Dog and Infant

Infants and dogs can do very little together. Therefore, both should only be brought together for brief sniffing contacts overseen by the parents. You can find out how to get an older dog used to a baby on page 32.

Dog and Creeping Baby

Crawlers are conquerors. The dog is also one of the new experiences and will in the truest sense of the word be "grasped." This means that close watching is necessary because crawlers pull painfully on fur and poke their fingers into dogs' eyes. Therefore, the dog and crawler must only be allowed to meet under careful supervision.

Dog and Toddler
Drawing 1

The relationship between an adult dog and a two- to three-year old child becomes less and less complicated. Therefore, the parents only need to supervise now and then when dog and child play together.

Dog and Kindergarten Child
Drawing 2

Now the child can undertake small jobs. She might lead the dog on the leash, but always while a parent keeps the end in his hand. The child may also help with feeding, but keep in mind that the dominance order (see page 16) comes to bear especially strongly during feeding. Explain to your child that she may certainly offer the food dish but may never take it away

2 At kindergarten age the child may already hold onto the dog's leash.

3 The school child takes over the first jobs: He can give the dog his filled food dish.

Short List of Behavioral Guidelines
• Children under the age of nine should never walk a dog unaccompanied.
• After the age of ten, the child can take a well-trained small to medium-sized dog walking alone in familiar territory.
• Only children older than fourteen may take larger dogs walking alone.
• Take into consideration that you are entirely responsible and liable for accidents that are caused by your dog!

again as long as the dog has not finished her meal.

Dog and School-age Child
Drawings 3 and 4

Now the child has reached an age that makes it possible to take increasing responsibility for the dog. The grade school child can offer the food dish alone, because the dog knows from positive experience that her food will not be competed for by her pack mate (see drawing 3). An older school child, from about eight years old, can brush the dog's coat by herself, and the child can also assist with bathing the dog (see drawing 4).

Walking the dog: When determining when a school child can go walking with a dog, you need to take into consideration the size of the dog, his temperament, and his aggressiveness. The dog's leadability and the degree of training he's had is also very important. A nine-year-old child of average physical development as a rule has no difficulties with a good dachshund (or comparable dog), while a temperamental boxer (or a dog of similar size) can definitely lead to problems.

If many other dogs are in the area where the dog is being walked, there can also be fights, for not all dogs get along with each other. The child must under no circumstances interfere (see "Play Fighting," page 52). Females in heat or sick dogs change their character and, thus, should not be walked by children under the age of fourteen without being accompanied by an adult.

Issuing commands: Make sure that your child does not try to imitate you and give the dog commands. They will not necessarily be carried out because the dog ranks the child lower in dominance order (see "Dominance Ranking in the Family," page 16). Children must never demand obedience from the dog. The following of the command requires strict subordination from the dog, which he will show to the child but not always willingly.

4 With grooming the child takes on a responsible job.

31

The first days: Of course your children may also have contact with the dog in the first few days, but only under your supervision. The children can play with her several times a day and also take her in their arms briefly. But keep the little dog from being pulled around among the children. Play with the puppy shouldn't last more than five to ten minutes per session at the beginning, because the little animal needs time to rest. How often and how long your children can play with the puppy in the first few days depends on how fast she gets acclimated and loses her shyness.

The first nights: At night the puppy will probably make her loneliness known with howling or wailing. She will miss the warmth of mother and brothers and sisters very much. You and your children should not take the puppy into bed with you, because once she has enjoyed the privilege, she will want to continue to get into the bed.

My tip: To make the first nights easier for the puppy, you can lay a hot water bottle and an alarm clock wrapped in a hand towel in the crate. They replace the warmth of former pack and the heartbeat of the mother dog.

Don't Rush the Older Dog

An adult dog needs much understanding and restraint; she will probably grieve for a while for the "lost pack," to which she had a strong attachment. The older the dog is, the more strongly she will suffer and thus the longer the adaptation to her new family will take.

My tip: Don't make too many demands on your new dog with too much fussing. Show her the crate and keep your children back a little. They shouldn't rush at her right away. Your dog should get to know her new surroundings in peace and experience the moods and movements of the family members. She will soon take the initiative, lay her muzzle on a knee, and thus signal that it is now time for a few petting sessions.

Getting the Dog Used to a Baby

Because the growth of a family cannot be explained to the dog, she suddenly sees herself confronted with a new situation when her mistress comes home from the hospital one day with a new baby. To keep the dog from developing a bad relationship with the infant and regarding the baby as an intruder in her territory, you should observe a few rules.

Prepare the dog for the baby: Even during the pregnancy you should practice certain behavior patterns with the dog that will later be demanded of her.
• If the nursery is going to be off limits for the dog after the arrival of the baby, you absolutely must establish the future prohibition in advance. So, several weeks ahead of time, strictly forbid your dog to enter the room. Thus, she will not connect it with the baby later.

Who wouldn't love this funny little puppy?

An infant's first contacts with the dog should always take place under supervision.

- Allow your animal to sniff quietly at the crib and also the baby carriage. Dogs are curious and like to get familiar with new furniture.
- If the dog sees her mistress as "pack leader," the master should take care of the dog more, the closer the due date comes. The sorrow of the dog during the absence of her mistress in the hospital won't be so bad if she has already gotten closer to the master than before.

The baby comes home: So that your dog accepts the baby as a member of the family, she should have as many contacts with the baby as possible.
- When the master brings mother and baby home from the hospital, the dog should have been prepared in advance. Make sure that the new mother takes a little time with the dog after she gets home. Help the dog adjust to this subtle change in her pack and the new member of it. Soon the dog will welcome the new little human.
- At home you should thoroughly introduce your dog to the new family addition. Hold the baby near the dog so that your pet can look at your baby and take in its scent. Giving it lots of praise when she behaves well will help her to accept the new member of the pack.

Everyday life with a dog and a baby: You should include the dog in everyday events.
- When the baby is in his room, the dog already knows that she must stay outside. Calmly leave the door open while you settle the tiny addition in his new home. Dogs are very curious and want to take part in the happenings in the pack. This way the dog can get used to the unfamiliar sounds made by the new family member and get them into her mind as normal noises for the future.

33

HOW-TO: Playing with the Dog

For children, playing with a pet dog is especially important. Together they will learn each other's preferences and limitations and learn to appreciate each other.

The Right Playthings

The pet store offers a wide variety of dog toys. These should be made of natural materials, rather than of plastic, and should not be painted, glued, or chemically treated.

Gnawing toys are important for puppies. Some toys to consider are chewing ropes, pulling rings, untearable cloths, and sturdy pieces of wood with rounded corners that won't splinter; these toys will withstand sharp puppy teeth, and will satisfy the chewing drive. All dogs love chewing bones of rawhide. Unsuitable toys are ones made of metal, soft plastic, and painted wood.

Balls should be made of hard rubber and be appropriate to the size of the dog. Absolutely unsuitable are balls of soft leather and plastic, which can tear or break and can be swallowed.

Squeaky toys are much beloved by dogs. However, the toys must withstand the dog's teeth and you must be careful because the built in "squeakers" can be swallowed.

Ball Games
Drawing 1

Whether at home or on vacation, most dogs love ball games. Children have the same stamina to either throw the ball or to roll it as dogs do to tirelessly bring it back. The dog can be allowed to run outdoors, though of course only in a fenced yard or in a big field where there is no danger of the ball going into the street and the dog running after it.

Keep an eye on your children because they often know no moderation or limit when they are playing a game. This stressful play and fitness training should not overtax the animal's capability, especially during hot weather.

Tugging Games

An old, tearproof cloth of cotton or a pulling rope (from the pet store) are well-suited to tugs-of-war (see drawing, page 11). The dog pulls on one side and the child or grownup pulls on the other. But please pull with care or the dog's teeth can be injured in the heat of competition. A thick rope that won't split and doesn't have any sharp-edged plastic fibers can also be used.

Fetching Games
Drawing 2

Many dogs fetch with passion and endurance. Many things are suited for fetching, like balls, sticks, blocks of wood, or old socks. However, consider what you allow your dog to fetch, because he cannot make any distinction between old and new. And sometimes it can

2 Many dogs love the water and love to fetch little sticks out of the lake.

1 Ball games are good for fitness. This Shepherd dog chases joyfully after the ball.

happen that the dog will mix up the baby's squeaky duck with her own toys.

Play in the water: On an excursion to the lake, the dog can fetch a stick or a fetching toy from the water (see drawing 2). You should supervise your children while they are doing this and you should avoid currents when throwing things into the water for the dog. You should also avoid steep banks.

Please be careful and anticipate rocks, sharp objects, or a shallow bottom under the surface of the water, because the dog could injure herself while jumping in!

3 In his own sandbox the dog can burrow and root to his heart's content.

Games in the Yard
Drawing 3

Every dog (and every child) treasures the asset of a yard where she can safely romp to her heart's content.

Hiding places: You can hide treats, toys, or similar things among leaves, in tubs, and under outspread newspapers and give the dog a "search command." Also, children can play hide-and-seek with the dog: one child will lead the dog away while the other hides behind a tree or a wall. As soon as the child is out of sight, the dog will get her command to search.

Sandboxes: If you fear for your rose garden, you should set up a sandbox for your digging-crazy dog where she can rummage and root to her heart's content (see drawing 3). Train her to avoid the flower beds and the children's sandboxes for her burrowings. Bury toys in the dog's sandbox, let her look for them, and then praise her extravagantly.

Endurance Training
Drawing 4

Anyone who loves sports will find an unflagging companion in a dog.

Jogging: A dog can be an ideal partner for jogging. However, only older children should run with the animal on a leash. This way both the child and the dog can exercise equally and let off steam. Jumping over hurdles together (always of an appropriate size for the size of the dog) makes the whole thing even more fun (see drawing 4).

Bicycle riding: Larger dogs, especially those who love to run, can be led on a leash beside a bicycle. Reasonable endurance training doesn't hurt the dog, but she must learn to run on the roadside away from traffic. The distance should be increased slowly, according to the condition of the dog. Here, too, only older children should exercise with the dog.

Note: Neither play in the yard, nor jogging, nor running beside a bicycle can take the place of the daily walk, when the dog meets other dogs and can sniff as much as she wants.

Excursions to the country: The dog is especially happy to accompany her family on hikes in the woods, near the lake, on the beach, or in the mountains, and on other excursions into the country. During these times, she is with "her" pack the entire day and at the same time has a chance to get to know a new environment and take in many interesting smells.

4 Running across fields together and jumping hurdles is fun for both.

Grooming deepens the bond between a child and a dog.

Soon the baby is nothing special as far as your dog anymore. The new member has been taken into the pack and is completely integrated into the life of the dog.

Caution: You should have the dog thoroughly examined by a veterinarian and wormed five weeks before the baby is due. This will relieve any concerns about hygiene when your dog has contact with the baby. You should never leave the dog alone with the infant. Danger for the baby could arise through expressions of love or curiosity from the dog (for instance, tipping over the carriage or pulling at the changing table).

Developing Responsibility in a Child

A dog has a great teaching influence on a child because the meanings of responsibility and caring are introduced very naturally through him.

"That's my dog." This feeling fills every child with pride and strengthens him in his desire for independence. Sometimes a child will undertake burdensome duties to show parents that he is old enough to care for an animal.

When your child promises you to care for the dog "all alone," he means it, too. However, you must not let him do it completely alone. Any child, depending on his age, can undertake larger or smaller tasks in caring for the animal, provided that you supervise, support, and direct at the beginning (see "HOW-TO: Contact with the Dog," pages 30 and 31).

"My dog is feeling fine." For the dog to feel happy with herself in the family, the child should learn, early on, the meaning of proper animal care. This primarily consists of recognizing and satisfying the needs of the house pet. Explain to your child, for example, that the dog needs water right now because

- When you feed the child, diaper it, or talk to it, let your dog be there. She may also sniff quietly. The baby certainly isn't going to suffer any harm from it. Talk to the dog, too, so that she doesn't feel excluded.
- When you walk your baby in the carriage, take your dog with you on a leash. Nothing persuades a dog so much of the normality of her life as when she is allowed to go walking. Well-trained dogs quickly get used to trotting along beside the baby carriage.

she is thirsty. The child can easily understand this need, because he doesn't like to be thirsty either. Also, the pleasure that brushing the dog's coat gives is easy to explain. The dog is also prompted to respect the child more according to how much responsibility for the animal the child takes on. This is then expressed in greater affection and later also in a kind of voluntary obedience to the child.

Not Overburdening with Duties

It is very important to increase the child's responsibilities in small steps. Even if the child firmly makes up his mind to, he can never take on the entire responsibility for the care of the dog all by himself. He shouldn't be so overburdened by the tasks that he loses pleasure in caring for the animal or develops feelings of hate because he has no more time for other favorite activities (such as sports or playing with friends).

My Advice to Parents

Don't demand of your child what he can't do; let him learn gently. Rejoice over every step forward your child makes on the road to independence and show him that you are proud of him. This way the child learns that responsibility is not a heavy burden and that it also brings pleasure and leads to contentment and success.

The Child Refuses to Do His Jobs

One day, what you have feared from the beginning may happen in your family. The excitement of the new pet is gone, and the child has had enough of responsibility. Parental reproaches like "I knew all along that it was all going to land on me" or "We'll get rid of the dog if you don't care about it anymore" will not make

"Sinbad, can you tell me how to paint a dog?"

the child get back his lost sense of responsibility.

Find out the reason: React sensibly if your child suddenly no longer has any desire to do his part in caring for the dog. Punishment and scoldings usually only intensify the frustration and are not solutions. Talk quietly with your child and analyze the cause of the problem: What are the reasons for my child's behavior? Is the child being kept from other activities he likes by his dog-care jobs? Is the child under special (academic) stress at the moment?

Suggested solutions for parents:
- The child is overchallenged: Take the time-consuming jobs away from the child. In exchange, give him smaller duties that he can carry out conscientiously.
- A situation has changed for the child (higher academic demands, joining a sports team or a youth group): Reapportion the tasks within the family.
- The child is underchallenged: The area of responsibility handed to him is alone on a plateau that the child feels is always the same boring level of a job. Give your child new duties that again make the care of the dog exciting and interesting.
- The child is imitating his parents: Perhaps you have given the dog too little attention yourself and let him "get along on his own." Children often imitate the behavior of their parents. Practice your function as a positive example again and show your child what responsible and conscientious care of an animal is.

Caution: Under no circumstances should the animal suffer from the child's neglect. If need be, the parents should take full responsibility for taking the best care possible of the animal from now on.

When the Dog Causes Problems

Sometimes a dog suddenly develops unlikeable habits that are not tolerable in the family. You should research the cause. In most cases the grounds for the animal's misbehavior lies in your own faults in maintaining the dog. The more liberally you, as "pack leader," handle the management of the dominance order (see page 16), the more the dog presumes, because she will keep trying to reach a higher level. This begins with begging at the kitchen table and ends with showing her teeth threateningly when she just doesn't have any desire to carry out an order.

Rectify training errors yourself: You need to resolve to always react the same way in particular situations. Once you have permitted the dog to do something, it must always be permitted. What was once forbidden also must remain taboo. Only the necessary measure of consistency will make the dog ready to subordinate himself (see "Training Ground Rules," page 40). Basically, the rule is that all training measures are exclusively the province of a higher-ranking individual, like an adult.

Find an obedience class: Obedience classes are thoroughly suitable to help get the neglected education of the dog back on track (see "Dog Schools," page 46). However, you must also practice there with your dog. You need to use the commands and directions of the trainer so you don't confuse your dog with other commands.

Find a new home for the dog only as a last resort: In more serious cases—for instance, if your dog won't obey anymore at all or even bites seriously—

Digging in the sand together doubles the pleasure for the child and the dog.

it may be necessary to give the dog away. Explain to your child that your dog may do better in a different environment and find a new home for the dog. You should give her to an animal shelter only as a last resort.

Of Growing Old and Dying

A dog also grows older and slower over the course of years. Depending on the breed, the normal life expectancy is between eight and fifteen years.

The first signs of age: As soon as the capabilities of the dog change, her care should change accordingly. Even an old dog needs to have daily exercise. However, her high spirits are reined in and her need for rest is greater. This should also be explained to and respected by the children. Play is now limited by the capabilities of the dog. If she is tired or has no more desire to play, the game should end.

The last trip to the veterinarian: When the burdens of age become too heavy for the animal, you should be rational and kind enough to let the animal lay down her burden. However difficult the leave-taking is for the family and for the children, it would be wrong not to tell them about the illness or the approaching death of their four-legged friend. The shock of learning it is even greater after it has already happened. Therefore, include your children, depending on their ages, in this last segment in the dog's life. The grief won't be any less, but the feeling of having spared a beloved friend great pain is comforting.

The dog should make her last trip alone with her "pack leader." The family says good-bye to the dog at home. Hold her in your arms when she receives the lethal shot. Then she can go to sleep peacefully. You owe your faithful friend this service for all the long years she has brought you joy.

A new dog in the house: The emptiness a departed dog leaves behind is huge. The only real comfort may be to get a new dog, who crowds stormily and clumsily into your family's hearts. The right time for that is something every family must determine for itself according to its own feelings.

Training the Family Dog

So that the dog knows what he may and may not do, all members of the "family pack" should abide by the rules established at the beginning.

Obedience Is Important

The dog—like his ancestor, the wolf—is a pack animal and needs a leader whom he can respect, follow, and obey. Within the "human pack" (which is to say, your family) someone has to take over this lead position and control the dog with consistency and, now and then, with authority. Your four-legged friend will accept this if he is used to it from the beginning. Training a dog does not mean to force him into "slavish" obedience. Rather, the dog should respect "his" people and obey because of this respect.

My Advice to Parents

Children like to command the weaker family members when you are not there (no matter whether they are younger siblings or the dog). Explain to your children, however, that they are not allowed to train the dog. Requiring a dog to obey commands subordinates him. Because the dog lives according to a firm order of dominance (see page 16), he of course submits to anyone higher in rank. He may follow a command from a child, who is, to the dog, an equal or a subordinate, but not always accurately. If the child then tries to compel obedience from the dog (for instance, through scolding or blows), the dog can make his higher rank clear to the child (see page 17).

Therefore it follows that: children under fourteen years of age may not train the dog.

Training Ground Rules

To ensure that the training of your dog will be completely successful, all family members should take some basic rules to heart.

Only one person trains! Agree on who in the family is going to take over the training. Usually this task falls to the person who usually takes care of the dog because the animal learns more easily when he at first receives commands only from his "pack leader." Later the rest of the family members (only children over fourteen) can practice with the dog.

Consistency is imperative! One of the most important principles in dog training is consistency. Your animal expects clear rules that he can follow. Therefore, discuss with your family what the dog may and may not do. It only confuses the dog when he is allowed something one time that is strictly forbidden some other time. This confusion can be compounded if the conflicting rules come from different family members.

Use clear commands! Also discuss the commands you intend to use. The dog will recognize them only if all use the same orders. Everything else will confuse him. All orders must be short and concise.

Practice regularly! Only when you repeat the practice drills regularly will there be noticeable success in training your dog. Don't allow too much time between the individual lessons or your dog will have forgotten the commands by the next practice session.

A well-trained dog trots nicely along beside the stroller without pulling.

HOW-TO: Training

Training a dog demands time, patience, and empathy. The trouble will be worth it, though, for a well-trained dog is a joy to all around him. This section gives a short overview of the most important drills. Furthermore, you should read the comprehensive literature on the training of dogs (see page 62).

1 Every dog must learn to walk on the leash without pulling.

Leading
Drawing 1

Walking on a leash is an important drill that the young dog must learn as early as possible, but without pressure. First let him wear a light collar in the house, an hour at a time. When he has accepted that, take him on the leash. He will certainly struggle against this "loss of freedom" and pull against the leash. Then playfully pull the puppy to you bit by bit. Give the dog a little treat as a reward. You should avoid hard jerking or pulling on the leash so the puppy doesn't develop any unnecessary dislike of the leash. If you have some patience, it will soon work.

The Command "Come"

First practice this with the puppy on the leash. With the leash in one hand, crouch a short distance in front of him, call his name, and enticingly give the order "Come." If he runs to you, smother him with praise. A rewarding tidbit works real wonders. If he doesn't obey, pull gently on his leash but don't scold him if doesn't come right away. As the second step of the drill, fasten a thick fishing line 10 feet (3 meters) long to his collar, then call the puppy as soon as he turns away. If the dog doesn't obey the command, repeat the command and then pull gently on the fishing line. Then praise him as if he had come of his own free will.

The Command "Sit"
Drawings 2 and 3

Press the standing puppy's rear end down gently with one hand and command "Sit." While doing so, lay the palm of the other hand supportingly under his chest so that he doesn't run away or lie down (see drawing 2). You can also

2 In practicing "Sit," the puppy's rear end is gently pressed to the ground.

practice while you stand in front of your dog with the filled food dish in your hand that you hold in such a way that the puppy must look up. At the same time say "Sit" (see drawing 3). Your dog will automatically sit so he can look up more comfortably. Wait a little before you give him the food and don't forget to praise him.

The Command "Heel"

At this command the dog should walk along beside you at the pace you determine. Only start practicing this when your puppy is at least six months old. First let him romp until he is tired. Then put him on a short leash and start walking. When you start walking, give the command "Heel." After a few yards, stop, let the dog sit down, and praise him a lot. After the dog has learned the basics of this command, work directional changes into the drill.

3 While the puppy is looking up at his food dish, he automatically sits down.

The Command "Lie Down"

The goal of this drill is for the dog to lie down and only get up again when he is commanded to. This drill demands much discipline, so the dog should be at least nine months old for it. Give the leashed dog the command "Lie Down" and, while saying it gently, pull his front feet forward so that he must lie down. With the other hand, gently press on his shoulder. Then repeat the command and keep holding the dog to the floor. When he has understood that he should stay lying down, move a few steps away and keep saying several times "Lie Down." If the dog stands up without permission, move him back to the starting position and begin the drill all over again. Don't forget to praise him when he responds to the command properly.

The Command "Stay"
Drawing 4

At the command "Stay" the dog should remain at the spot where he was stopped with "Sit" or "Lie down." After the leashed dog is sitting or lying down, give the command "Stay" and at the same time move a few steps away from him. Reinforce the command with the signal of the raised right palm. Your dog may not follow you until you call him again with "Come." If he moves before that, place him firmly back at the same spot he was in before. At first it's enough if he only stays in place for a few seconds but gradually the length of time should be longer and the intervals should be increased. Praise your dog a great deal when the drill goes well.

Staying Alone

It is not right to leave a dog by himself for many hours every day. However, a young dog must learn to stay alone for a certain time. First practice after play, when your dog is tired. Give him a chewing toy that he can occupy himself with. Then leave your apartment for about fifteen minutes with the command "Stay." If the dog keeps quiet, praise him. If not, scold him briefly and concisely and repeat the drill. Bit by bit increase the time spans before you come back. But then clearly show your pleasure at seeing him again.

The Dog and Riding in the Car

Any dog should be able to ride in the car. At first just sit your animal in the car for a short time and then give him a treat there. Get him used to the sound of the engine without driving. Only when he has lost his shyness can the first ride of a few hundred yards, at most, be taken, at the end of which a pleasant experience (for instance a meadow to play in) awaits him. You would be wise to have the dog travel in a carrier or crate so that he won't be tossed around and injured.

4 The raised palm supports the command "Stay." The dog may only leave his place when he is ordered to.

On a walk, the dog gets to sniff extensively.

- Don't overburden the puppy. He still needs a great deal of sleep. So end the drills when you see that his desire to play and his concentration are clearly waning. And don't ask anything that is beyond his capacity to grasp. Give him easy tasks and praise him when he does them well.
- Up to six months of age, two to three drills spread out through the day are enough.

Generally, the training sessions will increase later.

Training the Adult Dog

The older the dog is, the more difficult his training is. It's helpful if you know what training the animal had from his previous owner and what commands he knows. You should take over these commands. If the previous owner isn't available (for instance, with a shelter dog), you should try without pressure to make certain orders clear to the dog by means of rewarding snacks. Absolute reliable obedience is not likely to be accomplished in advanced age.

Praising and Scolding a Dog Correctly

A dog should be trained with praise and verbal correction, never with blows. Whether he does something right or wrong, your animal learns fastest when you praise or scold him right after the deed.

Praise: If your dog has followed a command well, show him your pleasure by praising him a lot and petting him. The dog thus connects the action desired by you with a reaction that is pleasant for him. With difficult drills, you can also give him a treat now and then. But that should not become the rule, or your dog will get used to carrying out the order just because of the treat.

Success Achieved in Small Steps

Give yourself enough time to train the dog and begin as soon as the puppy comes home to you. The time between the eighth and sixteenth weeks of life is very important for the mental development of the dog. During this time, he needs the daily contact with "his" people. Consider the following:

- The dog should learn gladly. You accomplish this best when the first drills are in the form of play and proceed without any pressure.

Scolding: Sometimes it's unavoidable and the dog needs to be punished. Your dog will only understand the reprimand, however, if it takes place directly after his misdeed.

The right way to punish: Usually it's enough to reprimand the dog with a sharp, loud "No" or "Ugh." You don't need to scream at all because, normally, a dog's hearing is very good. If this isn't enough, take your animal by the scruff of the neck and briefly shake him (see drawing, page 46). This is also how a mother dog controls her puppies.

What you must not do: Don't lift the dog off the ground when you shake him by the scruff of his neck. You can injure him that way. However, the front feet may be lifted off the ground a little.

Never call your animal to you after a misdeed to punish him. The dog doesn't remember what he did before but inevitably connects his coming with punishment. What's next but to learn from it that it's better not to come when called?

Don't Let Bad Behavior Become a Habit

What your animal is allowed and is not allowed is up to you. But remember that it's very difficult to root out bad behavior that a dog has made a habit. So pay attention to strict maintenance of all the rules from the beginning.

Beggers not welcome! A dog rarely learns faster than when it has to do with food. If he has ever understood that there was something to be gotten from the table, he will sit there with the endurance of a besieger and wait. Also, the fact that small treats can be snatched out of the hands of children doesn't take a dog long to discover. Therefore, never give him anything from the table, even if he whimpers ever so heartbreakingly and fixes you with a wheedling look. Entirely aside from this, human food is very unhealthy for the dog.

Jumping up is tiresome! People are usually not overjoyed when a dog jumps up on them. One reason is that they aren't always wearing old clothes on which the prints of dirty dog feet don't matter. Also, a big dog that jumps up on small children can make them fall and frighten them. Therefore, from the very beginning, don't let your

Obedience at street crossings is vital for a dog.

dog get used to jumping up. When you greet your four-legged friend bend over to him and then hold him firmly with both hands. But clearly show him your pleasure, speak in a friendly manner to him and pet him. Also, your children, friends, and relatives should greet the dog in this manner.

Sharp teeth hurt! A puppy has needle-sharp teeth and no inhibitions at all about using them. This has nothing to do with malicious pleasure or aggression. Rather, the teeth of the puppy play an important role in all dominance struggles among the littermates. Because the puppy will also nip your children, you should make it clear to the dog early on that he has to behave gently with humans. If he is carried away in total involvement in the next game and bites at your hand, press his upper lip between your hand and his teeth. This is simple and very effective because the puppy now feels the pinch himself. While doing this maneuver, warn him with an impressive command like "Careful" or "Be gentle." Practice often, for soon the command alone will be enough.

Dog Schools, Dog Clubs

Some dog owners are unsure whether they are training their dog properly. Anyone who doesn't trust himself to translate the training tips in dog books into action is well advised to look around for a dog club in his area that offers obedience training for beginners. You can get the name of dog schools in your vicinity from the American Kennel Club (see "Organizations," page 62).

My Advice to Parents

Check out the training program first before you enroll with your dog. Training methods that might be used for working dogs or guard dogs are not at all appropriate for family dogs. Under no circumstances should you allow yourself to be persuaded that your dog should be trained to attack people! This is sometimes called "schutzhund training" and is only for experts and not for family pets. A substantial reduction in the threshhold of the dog's inhibition against biting people is the consequence of such training.

The "sinner" is reproved by grasping skin at the back of his neck.

The Child and the Strange Dog

When children meet strange dogs, they should follow certain rules. Thus, conflicts can be avoided ahead of time.

Behavior with Strange Dogs

Conflicts do not usually arise in dealing with one's own dog but do happen more often with strange dogs. Children who have scarcely any experience with dogs or are afraid of them and not prepared for contact with them are especially affected by this. But also endangered are children who transfer their experiences with their own—good-natured and fully trusted—animal to other dogs. Not every dog is nice with children and so patient that he will tolerate anything. In particular, dogs who are not used to dealing with children or have already had bad experiences with children as puppies must be treated with corresponding caution. Parents should be aware of these problems and urge their children to observe some important behavioral rules when they come into contact with strange dogs (see "Small Book of Dog Etiquette," page 56).

The Territorial Behavior of the Dog

Where the meeting between dog and child takes place has a big influence on the aggressive reactions of dogs, because dogs are decidedly territorial. This trait can be clearly observed in males who leave their scent marking with the familiar lifted leg in areas they consider their territory (yard, empty lot, daily walking route) and thus signal to intruders that they are in charge of this region.

Why does a dog mark? A look at the wild dog pack offers enlightenment. The pack needs a sufficient hunting area with a quantity of game that ensures the survival of the entire group. In addition, the lead dog is the "lord of all females" and he allows no rivals on his turf. To make the boundaries of his own territory recognizable to a stranger to the pack, the territory is marked out with scent left at intervals. And any intruder who ignores these boundaries is relentlessly chased, because he can present competition for food and females.

The tame dog also has these wild instincts. This is why people who pass by the garden fence or visitors are barked at, and day in and day out mail carriers have a hard time walking unharmed through yards that are guarded by dogs.

Barking Dogs Also Bite

Everyone knows the old saying about a dog's bark being worse than his bite. In fact, there are dogs who have made barking their life's work and who, when things get really serious, run away with their tail tucked under. On the other hand, barking can also indicate that the dog does not regard the person encountered as a friend. Failure to respect this threat can quickly escalate to the next warning step—growling and raised back hair. If this signal is also ignored and the dog continues to be irritated, the next step can be a nip.

Advice to parents: Because children can never evaluate whether barking is "only noise" or the prelude to aggressive behavior, they should always take a dog's barking as a warning.

47

The dog plays just as happily and boisterously with the friend of "his" child.

Advice to children: Take barking seriously and don't annoy the dog further by imitating him. Go quietly past without taking any notice of him.

Contact with Dogs in Their Own Territory

"Beware of the Dog!" Because you never know how vigorously the dog on the other side of the fence defends his territory, in the interests of safety you should believe the warning sign on the garden gate.

Often children have fun by teasing a barking dog on the other side of a fence. Not only is the barking imitated in such cases, but the animals are shot at with water pistols or peashooters or even pelted with stones. Another favorite game is rattling sticks along picket fences.

Certainly the children are only full of high spirits and the fence lends them the deceptive feeling of being more than a match for the dog. However, the game is a dangerous one. Dogs don't jump over fences, as a rule. But what could happen if the gate happens to be open? The dog has a good nose and can easily identify the "little teases." And possibly—especially if he isn't very patient and good with children—he might take advantage of the opportunity and make it clear to the little "intruder" who the "lord of the territory" is by springing on the child while barking (see "When a Dog Becomes Aggressive," page 54).

Advice to parents: Make it clear to your children early on how a dog can react on his own ground. Describe how to behave with friendly dogs, too, who are lying quietly in their yard and napping. They are no less watchful and can become ready to defend in a moment's time.

Advice to children: It is better to cross the street than to irritate a barking dog unnecessarily by going past him. If passing this particular place can't be avoided, ignore the animal and don't deliberately irritate it further. Also, leave alone any dog that gives an entirely friendly impression. Don't speak to him and don't put your hand through the fence to pet him. He could possibly misunderstand it as an "invasion" of his territory and maybe even bite because he is defending it.

When Your Child Visits Friends

Your child may come into contact with a dog when he is visiting friends. Even then he should be prepared with the right way to treat a dog.

Advice for parents: Impress on your child that he should never play alone with a strange dog. He should play with a friend's dog only if the friend or the friend's parents are in the room. Teach your child the right way to behave with a dog (see "Small Book of Dog Etiquette," page 56)

Advice for children: Don't bother a dog anymore when he withdraws to his bed. He wants to sleep then and be left in peace. If he is busy with a bone or a toy, don't interfere. Let the dog eat and drink in peace. Don't bother him and don't take away the feeding dish. The dog will defend his "own" toys, bones, or food and bite you if he thinks you are going to take things away from him. When the family has a mother dog with puppies, wait until a grown-up from the family leads you to the mother.

Contact with Dogs on "Neutral Ground"

In fact, children meet strange dogs daily and everywhere on ground that is strange territory for both sides—usually in the streets of the city and in public parks or places that serve the community as relaxation areas. Here the interests of dog owners and concerned parents collide with each other. Unfortunately, some dog owners lack the insight to keep their animals out of the sandbox and to keep them leashed on lawns, playing fields, or in parks where mothers often walk with their children (see "Careless Dog Owners," page 54).

Advice for parents: Normally you can assume that dogs outside their own territory are not interested in unknown humans, because they have scarcely any territorial claims on "neutral ground." Nevertheless, you should make your children familiar with the most important behavioral rules in dealing with strange dogs (see the "Small Book of Dog Etiquette," page 56).

Advice for children: Don't call a strange dog. Stand there quietly if a dog runs up to you because he is only curious. Hold down the back of your hand for him to sniff (see drawing, page 55). He only wants to smell your scent briefly and then go on his way again.

The fetching stick is a "prey substitute" and a plaything in one.

HOW-TO: Avoiding Conflicts

This section pulls together an overview of all the most important behavior patterns for contact with strange dogs. If you as parents conscientiously educate your children as to how they are to treat dogs, most of the conflicts can be avoided ahead of time.

Dogs in Their Own Territory

Dogs are very territorial. Just like their wild relatives, they claim a territory for themselves and guard and defend it. Most dogs—exceptions to the rule are possible, of course—watch very alertly over this territory and endeavor to keep any intruder, including children, away from it more or less aggressively.

• Never leave children unsupervised in a strange place with an unknown dog. One never knows how intensely the dog defends his territory. Children should not anger or tease a dog watching from behind a fence.

• *Dogs in the car:* Many dogs also regard the family car as their own territory. Never stick a finger through a window opening to pet a dog in a car. Leave dogs in open cars alone.

Going to Visit Strange Dogs

Drawings 1 and 2

When children are visiting a family with a dog, they should take to heart the following rules of behavior:

The dog in his place: A dog who withdraws to his bed with a rawhide bone or a toy wants to be left alone and not be disturbed further.

• Children must respect the dog's resting phases (see drawing 1). After a rest the dog will certainly ask of his own accord to resume the joint game.

The dog at the food dish: Most dogs have no sense of humor when it comes to eating. Here the dominance ranking comes into play particularly strongly, and it can thus be expected that the dog will maintain his position against the stranger with energy.

• For children the already stated rule holds true: keep your hands off food dishes, gnawing bones, and treats.

A dog and her puppies: The ground rule is that a mother dog who is defending her young is capable of being extremely aggressive.

Cute little puppies have a powerful drawing power for children. But this attraction can be completely misunderstood by the mother.

• Children should never pick up puppies, hold them up, or take them away from the mother dog at all without supervision. Children should be lead slowly by an adult to the puppies (see drawing 2).

1 When the dog has withdrawn to his bed with his rawhide bone, the children must not bother him anymore.

2 Children may only approach a mother dog with puppies under the supervision of an adult.

50

Dogs on "Neutral Ground"

Beyond the borders of their range, dogs are far less territorial. As a rule children are scarcely noticed. However, some dogs come up curiously to sniff children.
- Basically, children should follow the rules in the "Small Book of Dog Etiquette" (see page 56) when they meet a strange dog.

Strange Dogs on a Leash
Drawing 3

The leash is a direct connection between a mistress or master and a dog. In some situations, this close connection also strengthens the animal's readiness to respond protectively. This is especially true in dusky light or at night.
- Keep children from rushing to a leashed dog unless you know the animal well and know that it will respond in a friendly manner.

3 Children should not run up to any dog but first ask the dog owner whether they may pet him.

Strange Dogs Tied in Front of a Store
Drawing 4

A dog tied in front of a store is in a particularly stressful situation because he is separated from his pack leader. As a rule he has no interest in being "comforted" by a strange child. His entire consciousness is focused on the return of his master or mistress. Special caution is required if the dog is tied beside objects belonging to his owner, for example a bicycle, baby carriage, or shopping bag. Since the dog is supposed to guard these possessions, he will inevitably regard any approach as a threat to "his possessions" and accordingly react aggressively.
- You should teach children not to go near dogs that are tied. When children enter the store, they should ignore the tied dog, not speak to it, and not stroke it.

Play with Dogs

Frequently you see small children playing in public parks with strange dogs without any adult supervision. This is careless in the extreme. No one can rule out that the child can come to harm through a false reaction or the nature of more aggressive dogs.

4 A dog waiting in front of a store should not be spoken to or stroked.

- Basically, small children should never play with strange dogs without supervision and without the express permission of the dog owner.

When Dogs Fight

Scuffling dogs are concentrating completely on their opponent and take no notice of children standing around. Should the child make the mistake of mixing into the fight, perhaps to stop it, it can lead to serious injuries.
- If children are in the vicinity of a dogfight, you should remove them immediately without any further intervention. The dogs will settle it by themselves.

Playing with Strange Dogs

Children love to play ball. Many dogs also share this passion. So conflicts can arise. For example: The dog owner throws a ball for his animal, which the dog joyfully brings back to him, and the child thinks that he is allowed to take part in this game. A dog will hardly give up his ball voluntarily. The animal doesn't need to react aggressively at all. Perhaps the child is just going to reach for the ball at the same time as the dog snaps at it. This can lead to painful experiences. Some dogs (Boxers, for example) also like to defend the ball with their front feet. Scratches from dog claws are also quite uncomfortable.

Advice for parents: Ask the dog owner if the child may throw the ball a time or so. Find out if there is any danger that the dog will defend his plaything "with tooth and claw."

Advice for children: Don't play with a strange dog if you don't see his owner in the vicinity. Ask beforehand if you may play with the dog and what games he likes.

Play Fighting

It often happens that strange dogs start fighting with each other in play. This may get quite rough and it seems from the outside looking in to be more dramatic than it actually is. The at-first harmless dog game can turn into a critical situation if a child whose dog is involved in such a sham fight interferes in the conflict in order to protect his own animal from the other "bad dog." Now the dogs' game can suddenly become serious, because the child's dog thinks he must protect his "pack mate" (the child). In their zeal the animals can no longer distinguish whether they are biting the other dog or the arm of the child. This is extremely dangerous!

Advice for parents: Instill in your children over and over not to mix into a dogfight under any circumstances.

If your dog has received bite wounds in a dog fight, you should immediately take him to a veterinarian as a precautionary measure. You may not know if the other dog has had rabies shots. If a human is even nipped or scratched, saliva from an unvaccinated dog could prove very dangerous. Medical precautions must be taken immediately!

Advice for children: Leave fighting dogs to themselves. Never try to get your own dog out of a brawl. Even if he is injured in the fight, you must under no circumstances and in no way come to the aid of your four-legged friend as long as the fight is in progress. Also, don't scream at the dogs while they are fighting—it only raises their aggressiveness—but wait quietly some distance away until the animals separate.

Dogs Tied in Front of Stores

A dog tied in front of a store, whether he protests against his loneliness by barking or howling or lies there quietly and waits, is always a temptation to sympathy. Children, especially, think they have to comfort him. Many children do not understand when the dog reacts apparently "ungratefully." However, a dog tied in front of a store can find himself in an outstandingly stressful situation, because "pack leader" has left him behind for a stretch of time. The dog finds the sympathy of strangers in no way reassuring; his loneliness becomes even more threatening for him because an unknown person approaches him and his human packmate is not there in order to help him. It is thus conceivable that such a dog may sometimes snap.

Even if he just looks so cute, the dog should not be fed from the table.

Advice to parents: Impress on your children that a waiting dog should always be ignored.

Advice to children: Don't speak to a waiting dog and don't go up to him to pet him. When you go into the store in front of which the dog is waiting, just pass him quietly.

Strays

Unfortunately, many irresponsible dog owners, out of laziness, simply let their dogs run without taking them for a walk. These dogs, often males, then wander all over the neighborhood. You often see them trotting along purposefully and not looking behind them for their owner like other free-running dogs. These dogs usually have a definite route that they follow daily. As a rule, you can generally assume that they are harmless, are concerned with their own business, and scarcely pay attention to any other people.

Advice to parents: If a stray regularly turns up at the playground, it is advisable to alert the animal control officer so that the dog can be caught and his owner can be informed.

Advice to children: Ignore stray dogs, don't speak to them, and don't bother them. Also, don't try to stop them or pet them.

When a Dog Becomes Aggressive

Someone who has little or no experience with dogs can hardly judge when a dog is really threateningly aggressive. Much is only show. Growling and barking can even be a sign of a good mood or the demand to play (see "How the Dog 'Speaks'," page 15; "HOW-TO: Body Language," pages 18 and 19).

If a dog threatens you: If you have the impression that a dog can become unfriendly, only extraordinary presence of mind will help. Panic reactions like hitting the dog, giving commands, or the like will only increase the animal's aggression.

What you can do: The most important rule is to keep calm and act in control. Don't run away; the dog is faster than you are. Your flight will only awaken his hunting instinct, and he will most certainly chase you. Rather, stand there silent and as motionless as possible. Don't look the animal in the eyes; that only challenges him to a measure of strength. If your child is crying in fear, take him in your arms to quiet him. In all probability the dog will lose interest after a time and run on.

What your child should know: As a precaution you should also teach your child not to stare in the dog's eyes in a dangerous situation, not to cry, and not to run away. In any of these situations, the danger that the dog will spring is large, and even the smallest dog is always faster than the child.

Naturally it is extremely difficult to make clear to a child that he should remain motionless when a dog becomes aggressive. The overpowering drive of fear urges to flight, but in this case it is the worst imaginable ploy to escape a threatening dog.

If the situation becomes serious: Should the gravest event ever occur (quite improbable), and a dog grabs you or your child in his teeth, it makes little sense to try to pull the clothing, arm, or leg out of his grip. The dog will only grasp more strongly. Even though it is very hard to do, the ideal reaction is to remain calm and keep still. Explain this to your child and impress on him not to cry loudly. Any resistance or shrill screams just stimulates the dog more. On the other hand, something that doesn't move and remains soundless quickly becomes uninteresting to the dog. There is a great chance that he will then let go of you or your child. This is the best way to limit the danger of injury.

Careless Dog Owners

Unfortunately there are also dog owners who have no consideration for those around them. Some refuse to leash their dogs even though they see that children are afraid of their animals. Others do not keep their dogs from relieving themselves in children's play areas or on sidewalks.

Talk with one another: If you should be in such a situation, have the courage to talk with the dog owner.

• Describe your children's fear and ask that the dog be leashed. Ask the dog owner if he would be willing to go walking with you and your child sometime. This would be a good opportunity to get familiar with the dog.

• Point out to a dog owner that playgrounds and sandboxes are taboo for dogs for hygienic reasons.

The neighbors' aggressive dogs: If you have definite evidence that there are aggressive dogs being kept in the neighborhood that represent a danger to your family, you should, in the interests of your children, take action. Address your written complaint to the government of the local community and give them the name of the dog owner. It is certainly advantageous if a large group of affected people bands together.

In a large apartment house, aggressive and actually dangerous dogs are especially unpleasant. If appeals to the dog owner are not effective in such cases, the only thing left is a complaint to the landlord. He is obligated to remove disturbances of the peace in the house and that includes a threatening dog. If the dog owner remains uncooperative, the landlord can possibly even terminate the lease after notice.

Damages: If you or your child have suffered an injury from a dog, either clothing dirtied or torn or even wounds inflicted, then as a rule you have the right to damages. The animal owner is usually obligated to pay in accordance with most local or county legal codes.

Curious and friendly, the dog sniffs the back of the boy's hand.

Small Book of Dog Etiquette

When we meet a strange person we introduce ourselves, shake hands, and make conversation. In short, we respect the other person and express our respect by following the rules of politeness.

Among dogs there are also firm rules that the animals normally observe with each other (except in the case of dogs that are wrongly imprinted). For the human to be able to live in harmony with his four-legged friend, he should also be familiar with the most important rules for dealing with the dog. This chapter gathers together some basic rules that absolutely must be followed because of their importance in dealing with dogs—especially in the contacts between dogs and children.

Show the same respect for the dog that you want him to have for you!

Children don't need to be afraid of the dog, because the majority of dogs are peaceable. But parents should make it clear to their children that they must respect the dog, his lifestyle, his possessions, and his nature.

Never take a dog's food away from him!

As a rule the dog only allows her "pack leader" to take her food away. She will fiercely defend her food against any others who try it. Since the dog views children as lower in the order of dominance than she is, they should let her eat in peace and never take away her food dish.

These two understand each other without any big words. What could be nicer than to enjoy the day with your best friend at your side?

Never take a plaything away from a dog!

Even small children cry when someone takes a toy away. Likewise, the dog develops an understanding of what belongs to her. Among these are chewing bones, rubber toys, or other playthings. Children should only take such objects away from her when the dog is presenting in an obvious demand to play (see "HOW-TO: Body Language," pages 18 and 19).

Never pull a dog by the tail or by the ears!

This rule is really obvious in itself. However, some dogs tolerate a great deal from small children in their own family pack, because they rank them as puppies. However, parents should make their children aware that not every dog is so patient. Dogs who are not used to children can respond very sensitively.

Never lift a puppy by its front paws!

Puppies are cuddly and feel soft when you take them in your arms, but you should never lift them up by the front legs. It hurts them because dogs have no collarbone. You lift a puppy properly by putting a hand under its chest and supporting its rear end with the other hand (see drawing, page 22).

Never scream in a dog's ear!

A dog normally hears very well. Therefore, loud noises also give her pain. Dogs who are not used to children may even react hostilely to children's screams.

56

A family bike expedition should not overchallenge your four-legged companion.

Never startle a sleeping dog!

Usually dogs sleep lightly. However, intermittently they fall into deep sleep and are completely carried away. If a sleeping dog is stepped on or bumped by playing children, she can snap in fear.

Never try to order the dog around!

The dog always feels that she ranks higher than a child. Thus she will only carry out a command the child gives her if she is in the mood to. A child should never try to enforce an order because he has seen his parents do it. The dog will refuse such "presumption" of the subordinate in her own way. Parents should explain to their children that certain commands that require great submission from the dog (for example, "heel," or "down," or "stay") are absolutely taboo for them.

If the child observes some rules, living with a dog will be harmonious and peaceful.

Never stare a dog in the eyes!

When dogs stare at each other with a fixed gaze it is a kind of measuring of strength between dogs of (supposedly) equal rank. When one looks away, she has given in. If the eye contact remains fixed, further gestures of threat follow. When a child stares a dog in the eyes, the animal can interpret it as a threatening gesture. Therefore, it's better to look the other way.

Never grab a dog by the muzzle!

This is a dominance gesture that only a higher-ranking individual may carry out. In the wild dog pack you can observe that a superior performs the so-called overbite (see photograph, page 17). She grasps the muzzle of the subordinate one with her own jaws and so shows her dominance. If a child grasps a dog by the muzzle, the dog can interpret this as challenge by one lower in rank and respond by nipping.

Never jump on a dog from behind, even in play!

There are children who like to try to ride on a dog, especially when it is a large one. Here caution is urged, for among dogs attempting to mount them from behind is taken as a gesture of dominance that may only be undertaken by those higher in rank. The dog can misunderstand the child's play and make her higher rank unmistakably clear by snapping.

Never run away from a leaping dog!

Curious dogs oftentimes have the habit of jumping up like wild animals. Often they bark at the same time. As a rule they do it out of joy and high spirits. It is completely wrong to panic and run away from them at this point!

There is great likelihood of falling down and getting hurt. Besides, it will only awaken the dog's hunting instinct. The best thing is to stand there quietly and let her sniff. When it gets too boring for the dog, she will run away again.

Never hit a dog!

Blows are completely unknown in the dog pack but are always experienced by the dog as aggression. It is therefore a basic rule that children (and of course adults too) should never—even in play—hit a dog or kick at him.

Never hold a dog back when his master is calling him!

When the "pack leader"—that is, the master or mistress—is calling the dog to him, the dog strives to obey. If she is held fast, perhaps in fun, by a child (that is a subordinate), the dog can try to free herself from this "trap" by snapping.

Don't talk to dogs that are tied!

Tied dogs are either waiting for their mistress or master or they are supposed to be guarding something. In either case they are not interested in strange children. On the contrary, they can respond extremely hostilely when children go to "comfort" them.

Don't tease dogs behind garden fences or in cars!

Dogs defend their territories, which include yards, cars, and houses. Sometimes children find it amusing to annoy dogs behind fences or in cars because it is fun when they bark like crazy. But a dog imprints with the scent of the child and is guaranteed to recognize him the next time, when perhaps she isn't locked in. It cannot be ruled out that the next time she may give the child a "lesson."

Let strays go on their way in peace!

Normally a straying dog has no interest in playing children. Therefore, it is best not to pay any attention at all to the animal. Under no circumstances should you run away screaming or should you even throw stones at the dog.

Index

Accidents, 10–11
Acclimation, 28–29, 32
Accommodations, 23–24
Active submission, 19
Age considerations, 21–23, 39
Aggression, 54–55
Aggressive breeds, 9–10
Aging, 39
Animal shelters, 23
Anxious mood, 18
Attack, signals before, 19
Australian Shepherd, 7
Automobile travel, 43

Babies, 30, 32–33, 36
Ball games, 34
Barking, 15, 47–48
Beagle, 7
Begging, 45
Behavior:
    problems, 45–46
    strange dogs, 47
Bicycling, 35
Biting, 10–13, 46–48
Body language, 18–19
Breeds, 7
    aggressive, 9–10
    dangerous, 8–9
    mixed, 22
Bull:
    Mastiffs, 9
    Terriers, 9
Buying:
    advice, 20–27
    time, 20–21

Car travel, 43
Children, interactions with, 28, 30–31
Clubs, 46

"Come" command, 42
Comforter, role as, 4
Commands, 42–43
    clear, 40
    issuing, 31
Communication, 15–16
    body language, 18–19
    vocal, 15–16
Conflicts, avoiding, 50–51
Consistency, 40
Crates, 24
Crying, 16

Dachshund, 7
Developmental phases, 14–15
Diet, 24, 26
Digging, 35
Display behavior, 18–19
Dominance ranking, 16–17
"Down" command, 43

Ears, 15
Endurance training, 35
English Springer Spaniel, 7
Equipment, 24
Etiquette, 56–59
Euthanasia, 39
Exercise, 26
Eyes, 15
    contact, 58

Family:
    behavior, 16–17
    considerations, 28–39
Fear, 6, 8
    overcoming, 8
Feeding, 24, 26
Fetching games, 34–35
Fights, 51
    play, 52

French Bulldog, 7
Friendly mood, 18

Games, 34–35
Golden Retriever, 7
Growling, 15

Health precautions, 26–27
"Heel" command, 42
Hiding, 35
Homecoming, 28
Housing, 23–24
Howling, 16

Illness, signs of, 26–27
Imprinting phase, 14
Infants, 30
Irritability, threshold, 9

Jogging, 35
Jumping, 45–46

Language, 15–16
Leading, 42
Leash:
    laws, 10
    training, 42
"Lie Down" command, 43

Maltese, 7
Marking, 16, 47
Mentality of the dog, 15
Mixed breeds, 22
Moods, 18
Muzzle, 58

Neutral ground, contact on, 49
Newborn phase, 14
Nipping, 46
Nose, 15

60

Obedience class, 38
Owners, careless, 54–55
Ownership considerations, 4, 20

Pack behavior, 16
Passive submission, 19
Pit Bulls, 9
Play, 26, 34–35
   invitation, 18
   mate, role as, 6
Pomeranian, 7
Poodle, 7
Praise, 4
Pug, 7
Punishment, 45
Puppy:
   diet, 24
   lifting, 56
   selection, 23

Ranking, 16–17
   phase, 15
   rules of, 12
Respect, 27

Responsibility, developing, 6, 36–38
Rottweilers, 9

Sandboxes, 35
Schnauzer, 7
Schools, 46
Scolding, 45
Selection, 21–22
Self-confidence, development of, 6
Shelter dogs, 23
Sheltie, 7
"Sit" command, 42
Sleep, 58
Sniffing, 16
Socialization phase, 14–15
"Speaking," 15–16
Squealing, 16
"Stay" command, 43
Strange dogs, 47–55
Strays, 53–54, 59
Submission, 19

Territorial behavior, 47–49
Toddlers, 30
Toys, 34, 56
Training, 40–46
   commands, 40, 42–43
   consistency, 40
   endurance, 35
   errors, 38
   leash training, 42
   practice, 40
   praise, 44
   punishment, 45
   rules, 40
   scolding, 45
Transitional phase, 14
Transportation, 28
Travel, 43
Tugging games, 34

Walking the dog, 31
Water games, 35
Whimpering, 15
Wolf heritage, 14

Yard games, 35

Useful Addresses and Literature

Organizations
American Kennel Club
51 Madison Avenue
New York, NY 10038
(212) 696-8200

Canadian Kennel Club
89 Skyway Avenue
Etobicoke, Ontario
Canada M9W 6R4

Registration of Dogs
Purebred dogs are often registered with the American Kennel Club.

Magazines
Dog World
29 North Wacker Drive
Chicago, IL 60606-3298
(312) 726-2802

Dog Fancy
P.O. Box 53264
Boulder, CO 80322-3264
(303) 666-8504

Books for More Help
American Kennel Club, *The Complete Dog Book* (Howell Book House, Inc., New York, 1992).

Alderton, David, *The Dog Care Manual* (Barron's Educational Series, Inc., Hauppauge, NY, 1986).

Baer, Ted, *Communicating with Your Old Dog* (Barron's Educational Series, Inc., Hauppauge, NY, 1989).

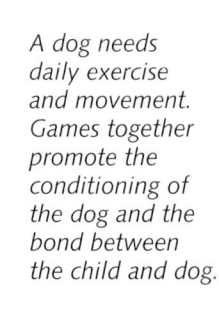

Baer, Ted, *How to Teach Your Old Dog New Tricks* (Barron's Educational Series, Inc., Hauppauge, NY, 1991).

Coile, D. Caroline, *Show Me!* (Barron's Educational Series, Inc., Hauppauge, NY, 1997).

Klever, Ulrich, *The Complete Book of Dog Care* (Barron's Educational Series, Inc., Hauppauge, NY, 1989).

Lorenz, Konrad Z., *Man Meets Dog* (Penguin Books, New York, 1967).

Pearsall, Milo, and Charles G. Leedham, *Dog Obedience Training* (Scribner's, New York, 1979).

Pinney, Chris C., DVM, *Caring for Your Older Dog* (Barron's Educational Series, Inc., Hauppauge, NY, 1995).

Pinney, Chris C., DVM, *Guide to Home Pet Grooming* (Barron's Educational Series, Inc., Hauppauge, NY, 1991).

Schlegl-Kofler, Katharina, *Educating Your Dog* (Barron's Educational Series, Inc., Hauppauge, NY, 1996).

Ullmann, Hans J., *The New Dog Handbook* (Barron's Educational Series, Inc., Hauppauge, NY, 1985).

Wegler, Monika, Dogs: *A Complete Pet Owner's Manual* (Barron's Educational Series, Inc., Hauppauge, NY, 1992).

Wrede, Barbara J., *Before You Buy That Puppy* (Barron's Educational Series, Inc., Hauppauge, NY, 1994).

Wrede, Barbara J., *Civilizing Your Puppy* (Barron's Educational Series, Inc., Hauppauge, NY, 1989).

A dog needs daily exercise and movement. Games together promote the conditioning of the dog and the bond between the child and dog.

Important Note
This book deals with the acquisition and maintenance of dogs. The author and publisher consider it important to point out that the maintenance rules in this book apply primarily to normally developed young animals of good breed lines, that is, to healthy animals of sound temperament. If you acquire an adult dog you must be aware that this animal has already experienced some character imprinting by humans. You should observe the dog especially carefully, including how he behaves toward people. If possible, you should also size up the previous owner. If the dog is from an animal shelter, the shelter personnel may be able to provide you with information about the dog's origin and character. There are dogs that are unreliable in their behavior because of bad experiences they have had with people and that may, perhaps, even have a tendency to bite. These dogs should only be taken by experienced dog owners. Even with well-trained and carefully supervised dogs, there is the possibility that they can damage other people's property or cause accidents. A comprehensive insurance policy is important for your protection. Some breeds and individual dogs may cause the premiums for this policy to increase. You should also be sure to carry out all the necessary immunizations and worming (see page 26) for your dog, because of the considerable health risk to people and animals. Some diseases and parasites can be transmitted to humans. If your dog exhibits any signs of illness, you should have him examined by a veterinarian.

The Author
Günter Huth, himself a dog owner and trainer, has been writing about dogs for years in nonfiction for magazines and textbooks and fiction for children's books. He also works as a freelancer in children's programming for regional television.

The Photographer
Christine Steimer has been a freelance photographer since 1985. She has specialized in animal photography and has been working for the magazine *Das Tier [The Animal]* since 1989.

The Artist
Renate Holzner is a freelance illustrator in Regensburg. Her broad repertoire extends from line drawings through photorealistic illustrations to computer graphics.

The photographs on the cover
Front cover: Children love dogs because they are true comrades and wonderful playmates.
Back cover: The dog is a part of everything "his" child does.

English translation © Copyright 1998 by Barron's Educational Series, Inc.

© 1996 by Gräfe und Unzer Verlag GmbH, München

Published originally under the title *Der Hund: Ein Freund für Kinder*

Translated from the German by Elizabeth D. Crawford
American Consultant: Joe Stahlkuppe

All rights reserved.

All inquiries should be addressed to:
Barron's Educational Series, Inc.
250 Wireless Boulevard
Hauppauge, New York 11788
http://www.barronseduc.com

Library of Congress Catalog Card No. 97-43005

International Standard Book Number 0-7641-0302-4

Library of Congress Cataloging-in-Publication Data
Huth, Günter.
    [Hund, ein Freund für Kinder.   English]
    The dog, a child's best friend : expert advice on mutual adjustment of child and dog / Günter Huth ; color photographs, Christine Steimer ; drawings, Renate Holzner ; translation from the German, Elizabeth D. Crawford.
       p.   cm.
    Includes bibliographical references and index.
    ISBN 0-7641-0302-4
    1. Dogs. 2. Children and animals. 3. Dogs—Social aspects. I. Title.
SF426.2.H8713   1998
636.7'0083—dc21   97-43005
                                                 CIP

Printed in Hong Kong
9 8 7 6 5 4 3 2 1

Even if the dog isn't invited inside the sandbox, at least he wants to sniff the children's "home-made delicacies" from the outside. Inclusion of the dog in children's play creates a positive stimulus for both the child and the dog.